NEBRASKA
SWEET BEETS

NEBRASKA SWEET BEETS

A HISTORY OF SUGAR VALLEY

....

Lawrence Gibbs

THE
History
PRESS

Published by The History Press
Charleston, SC
www.historypress.com

Front cover, top left: Colorado State University, Agricultural and Natural Resources Archive,
Archives and Special Collections; *top right*: Legacy of the Plains Museum Collection, Gering,
Nebraska; *bottom*: Legacy of the Plains Museum Collection, Gering, Nebraska.
Back cover: Colorado State University, Agricultural and Natural Resources Archive, Archives
and Special Collections; *inset*: from the author's collection.

First published 2020

Manufactured in the United States

ISBN 9781467144278

Library of Congress Control Number: 2020930472

This book is dedicated to my wife, Nita, who has always provided encouragement as I have pursued my dreams, and to my son Lawrence Matthew, who has inspired me with his success.

I also dedicate this to my late parents, Lawrence Alonzo and Minnie Dorothy Gibbs, who gave me the foundation that has helped me to succeed at most of what I have attempted in life.

Finally, to my late in-laws, Robert and Elvina Satur, who actually raised sugar beets in the Lake Alice community for many years and introduced me to the crop after I met their daughter.

CONTENTS

CONTENTS

ACKNOWLEDGEMENTS

'm not sure really where to start, as so many individuals and entities have assisted me in the research of this book. The story actually begins for me in the early 1970s, when I was fascinated to see that there were still steam locomotives operating in the United States every fall at the Great Western factories. I had been a train buff for many years, and steam in the 1970s was a rare sighting. That, plus the fact that my new in-laws raised sugar beets, kindled my interest in the industry. The unusual smell (to me at the time) of the refining process in the fall and the shift-change whistles and locomotive whistles seemed like an echo from the past. For the next forty or so years, I was too busy with family, career and politics to pursue further research. That changed after retirement, and the quest for the information to tell the story in this book began.

I know I will forget many who contributed to my research, but I'll try to list as many as possible who I can remember. I'll start with Craig Lind, who gave me a copy of a 1950 Scottsbluff County road map that showed in detail all the beet spurs that existed at that time. My research took me to Colorado State University in Fort Collins, as it is the repository of much of the historical information of the Great Western Sugar Company. I had the assistance of Linda Meyer and Vicky Lopez-Terrill at the Morgan Library. I had contact with Candy Hamilton, whose excellent book *Footprints in the Sugar* about Great Western (GW) primarily in Colorado and the people there inspired me to continue my quest to write a book on the sugar industry in the North Platte Valley. Pete Brown and others at Western Sugar in Scottsbluff were extremely helpful. Some photos and information came from rail historians Hol Wagner and Jim Ehernberger. Several photos Jim now has the rights to were taken by my friend the late Virl "Red" Davis of Scottsbluff. I had great help from the Legacy of the Plains Museum staff, including Amada Gibbs, Olivia Garl and Jordyn Bratton. Others who helped along the way included Jack Schmidt, Mike Zeiler, Frank Rogers, Sandra Hansen, Ken Middleton, Joan Johns, Library Director at Gering Diane Downer and the libraries and staff at Scottsbluff, Minatare, Torrington, Bayard and Grand Island and the Newberry Library in Chicago. Also of great assistance were the volunteers at the Western Nebraska Family Research & History Center in Scottsbluff. Needed information was also received from Ashley Brown at the Elkhorn Valley Museum. Thanks also to the *Bridgeport News Blade* and the *Torrington Telegram* for giving me access to their newspaper archives. Sarah Chaires at the Homesteaders Museum in Torrington was also very helpful. There are so many others who have helped, and I wish I could mention them all, but I must apologize to any I have forgotten. Your contribution to the book provided another piece of the most part long-forgotten puzzle, and it played an important part in the writing of this book. I have tried diligently to get all the facts correct with hundreds of hours of research. If I have made mistakes, please accept that I am only human, and that I tried. I hope I have succeeded for the most part. It is my wish that all who read it enjoy the story of *Nebraska Sweet Beets: A History of Sugar Valley*.

INTRODUCTION

This book is the culmination of many years of interest and several years of intense research. It was a project that I had time to seriously pursue only in recent years. It is not intended to be a comprehensive history of every aspect of the sugar beet industry in Wyo-Braska (a term used in the area to designate the eastern counties of Wyoming and the panhandle of western Nebraska) but is intended to tell the story of how it began here and what it took to get the entire infrastructure built to meet the needs of a rapidly growing agricultural crop industry. You will not find details on the people involved, as much of the story of the German-Russian, Japanese and Mexican people who provided much of the sweat that built a portion of the industry here has been covered in several other books.

What you will find here is a great deal of detail about what happened to get the industry started here, why it happened here, why it happened when it did and what transpired in the North Platte Valley in the first half of the twentieth century. A good portion of the information about the development of each of the factories in the valley was gleaned from many issues of local newspapers as well as other historical documents from the sugar companies, museums and libraries. The conditions that came together at the end of the nineteenth and early part of the twentieth centuries were just the right combination to cause an agricultural boom in the area with sugar beets. After mostly failure in the eastern part of Nebraska for sugar beets because of high humidity—and the related diseases it promoted—as well as the labor intensity of the crop and the opportunity for other crops, things were right for success in Wyo-Braska at that time. The completion of the early irrigation canals and their further expansion, good soil that was conducive to growing sugar beets, the arrival of the railroads, the semiarid climate and enough capital and labor to make all the pieces fit together were directly responsible for its development. "That a single industry should treble the population of the county, bring wealth to its inhabitants, and make its agricultural products the envy of the nation is scarcely conceivable."[1]

The previous quote, written in 1918, does not even take into account what would happen in the next decade or so in the area as that growth accelerated as a result of the industry's expansion. For a local town to have a sugar factory with plenty of acreage for beet production became the golden goose. As it was with so many booms, much of the sugar beet boom was short-lived. Over-expansion of processing facilities, combined with cheap foreign cane sugar allowed into the country by politicians who did not care about the domestic sugar industry, as well as two world wars, had totally different effects on the domestic sugar industry. Eventual competition for sugar from corn sweeteners as well as further competition from foreign producers had the effect of reducing the industry to just a small remnant of what it had been in the early twentieth century.

It is my hope that the information I have provided in this book will give people a better appreciation of the efforts it took to develop the North Platte Valley, at least in part because of the sugar beet industry. I think you will learn about many events, like the competition between the sugar beet giants and some of the smaller would-be competitors; and the starts and stops that caused great optimism in some communities, only to have those hopes dashed repeatedly before most finally achieved their goal of a sugar mill. The construction, expansion and eventual contraction of the importance of the railroad industry to the sugar beet industry are also examined with what I think is a great deal of information most are unaware of.

Most of all, I hope that if you are a history buff or just a casual observer who is curious about what happened in the North Platte Valley, you will be informed and entertained by the information I have presented here.

1

SUGAR

Humans have consumed some form of sugar for over a thousand years. The earliest sugar came from sugar cane grown mostly in the tropical regions of South Asia. Europeans developed a taste for sugar as a substitute sweetener for honey when it became available around the time of the Crusades, when samples of it were brought back to Europe when the crusaders returned from the Middle East. During the Middle Ages, a growing overland trade in sugar and other spices developed between Asia and Europe. This made sugar, along with other spices, available to the European market in limited quantities and at very high cost. After the discovery of the New World and the expansion of exploration seeking a cheaper trade route to Asia by sea rather than by land, the market for sugar grown from sugar cane expanded. As the European colonial powers established sugar plantations in the tropical regions of the New World, the cost declined. But it was still expensive in sixteenth-century Europe, because it had to be transported from the tropics by ship. This cost of transportation and a growing demand for the sweetener caused people to seek other plants that might provide sugar after refining and would be capable of being grown in the more temperate regions of Europe, not just in the tropics.

Sugar beets were as yet not widely known. They had been grown as a wild plant in Greece in the third century, and the product was used for medicinal purposes. "The beet was originally a wild plant of low sugar content. Probably more by accident than design it finally reached the sugar content stage where Oliver de Serres in 1590 A.D. noticed that the juice on boiling yielded a sugar syrup. He was looking for a material to make alcohol."[2]

Over the years, sugar beets have been selectively raised for greatly increased size and sugar content. The sugar beet (*Beta vulgaris*) has been bred to a size of up to about two pounds each from the skinny roots of its wild ancestor. While cane sugar has been commercially produced for over a thousand years, beet sugar has been in the commercial market for only about two hundred. The first sugar beet processing factory was built around 1800 in Europe. Sugar beets were introduced into the United States in 1830, and the first processing facility was built in 1838 in Massachusetts. The industry expanded to the western United States in 1852, when farmers started growing sugar beets in Utah. "By the year 1911 the beet sugar industry had passed the older cane sugar refining in supplying the world's sugar needs, the production of cane being 9,432,118 tons and of beet 9,587,588 tons."[3]

World War I had a tremendous effect on the sugar beet industry. It stopped most of the production in Europe and made it difficult to export the crop there from the United States. This greatly reduced supply led to a boom in sugar beet cultivation, sugar beet production and the beginning of overbuilding of sugar beet factories in the United States. The Nebraska Panhandle and Wyoming have multiple examples of this overbuilding, which eventually led to the decline of the industry in those areas.

THE SUGAR BEET INDUSTRY
IN THE UNITED STATES

Beet culture is now well entrenched in 18 states extending from California to Ohio. There are three main divisions of beet territory—the Pacific coast area, California to Washington—the Rocky Mountain territory comprising Utah, Idaho, Montana, Colorado, Wyoming, Nebraska and Kansas—and the eastern area comprising Minnesota, Iowa, Wisconsin, Michigan, Indiana and Ohio. The Rocky Mountain territory led in production with 450,000 acres devoted to beets.[4]

The first sugar beet company known to exist in the United States was the Northampton Beet Sugar Company in 1839 in Massachusetts. Although not successful (it closed after the 1840 campaign), it did establish some of the early processing procedures that were later used by others. The failure was attributed to inferior beets.

The industry was in its infancy in the United States, and many companies would follow with mixed results after the Northampton failure. Many factories were built at the end of the nineteenth and in the early twentieth centuries. One might ask, why so many? Transportation and its cost was the primary reason. Moving beets to the factory and then the finished sugar product to the final consumer was costly. Many factories were built close to the area of beet production and also close to many of their respective final markets. A *Sugar Press* article, "The West's Relation to Sugar," states the following:

> Farmers remote from the centers of population suffer in competition
> with those favored by proximity to markets because of the handicap of

higher freight rates on their products. To at least partially overcome this disadvantage, they have sought to market the food products of their land in the most concentrated form. The sugar crop can be converted into its refined form within short radius of the farm and marketed with the minimum of disadvantage.[5]

These factors probably explain the reason that seven factories were built (and others considered) in an area of about seventy miles along the North Platte River in Morrill and Scotts Bluff Counties in Nebraska and Goshen County in Wyoming. How did the Sugar Beet industry begin in Nebraska? Let's examine that next.

THE SUGAR BEET INDUSTRY IN NEBRASKA

T he story of the sugar beet industry in Nebraska actually begins about 320 miles east of Scottsbluff. It begins in Grand Island in 1889. A man named H.T. Oxnard of New York City was interested in building a sugar beet factory somewhere in the Midwest. First National Bank president H.A. Koenig of Grand Island, Nebraska, worked to convince Oxnard that Grand Island was the place to build. In order to sweeten the deal for Oxnard, the Grand Island Improvement Company, comprising about 150 local residents, raised about $100,000 to help finance the project. Additional financial incentives were provided when the state legislature passed a sugar beet bounty of one cent per pound of sugar produced in the state for the manufacturer.

GRAND ISLAND

Seed for sugar beets had been imported from France and Germany in 1888 and was planted in the central Platte Valley area that season to confirm the viability of growing the crop there. The planting and production was successful, and construction of the factory began in early 1889. Machinery for the plant was imported from France, arriving in the spring of that year. The Grand Island factory was the first sugar beet processing facility on the Great Plains and was the largest mill in the world in 1890.

AMERICAN SUGAR BEET FACTORY, GRAND ISLAND, NEB.

Above: American Sugar Beet Factory, Grand Island, Nebraska. *Vintage postcard. Author's collection.*

Left: Wagons arrive at Grand Island, circa 1900. *Legacy of the Plains Museum Collection, Gering, Nebraska.*

The company that Oxnard and Koenig formed was initially called the Oxnard Beet Sugar Company of Grand Island. By late September 1889, the factory was complete and the machinery installed, and they were ready to receive their first harvest of beets. Although the plant was designed to have a 350-ton slicing capacity, it took seven seasons to reach that goal. The plant became a part of American Beet Sugar Company in 1899 with the merger of four companies: the Oxnard Grand Island plant, the Norfolk Beet Sugar Company (Nebraska), the Chino Valley Beet Sugar Company (California) and the Pacific Beet Sugar Company (California). They eventually became known as American Crystal Sugar.

"Mountains of Sugar Beets at Grand Island Sugar Factory circa 1900." *Postcard in the Legacy of the Plains Museum Collection, Gering, Nebraska.*

The factory underwent expansion in 1915 and again in 1937–38. Major renovations in 1917 raised slicing capacity to about 1,200 tons per day. Another update happened in the 1950s as the plant converted its steam-operated machinery to electric operation. By 1959, the Grand Island mill was the smallest of all the factories operated by American Crystal. As with most of the factories that operated for many years, the Grand Island mill was serviced by a number of beet dumps in south-central Nebraska. Beet dumps were located at Gothenburg, Cozad, Lexington, Overton, Elm Creek, Kearney, Buda, Gibbon, Shelton, Denman, Wood River, Aurora and Fairfield. It's possible that there may have been others in the seventy-year history of the Grand Island factory. As with most of the factories on the Great Plains, the first harvests were moved from the dumps mostly by rail wherever possible. In later years, trucks replaced much of the rail hauling.

A unique fact about the Grand Island factory is that, for many years, from the 1890s through about 1960, it served the National Weather Service and kept official weather records for the area. The factory operated successfully for many years, but several problems eventually caught up with the plant. One was cercospora leaf spot disease, a fungal disease that attacks the leaves of many types of plants, with particularly detrimental effects on sugar beets. The fungus flourishes in high-humidity areas like central and eastern Nebraska. This became a widespread problem over the years, diminishing the amount of quality beets that could be harvested. (The dryer, semiarid high plains areas of the North Platte Valley have problems with the disease, but at a much lower incidence.) By the early 1960s, the factory's machinery was obsolete and wearing out, the beet crop quality and tonnage were decreasing and the plant was nearing the end of its useful life without another major update. The previously cited problems of quality and quantity of beets, combined with the major cost that another update would require, the declining price of sugar and the small size of the mill, led to the decision to cease operations in Grand Island at the end of the 1964 campaign. The seventy-four-year history of the first sugar factory on the Great Plains of the United States had come to an end.

NORFOLK

The second factory in Nebraska was opened by the Norfolk Beet Sugar Company in 1891. Construction started in 1890, after the Grand Island mill had been opened successfully. The plant was served by the Sioux City & Pacific Railroad and it quickly became a vital part of the community's economy. To facilitate the transportation of workers to and from the factory, a streetcar line was even constructed.

A group of local promoters had raised $150,000 to help secure the construction of the plant. Norfolk's plant avoided some of the construction problems that had occurred at Grand Island, as the developers were able to build on the lessons of that mill's construction and avoid many of the earlier mistakes. This main part of the plant occupied a site of about 50 acres on a total site of about 240 acres.

Sioux City and Pacific train at the Norfolk Sugar Factory, 1890s. *Photo from Mary M. Cornwall courtesy Elkhorn Valley Museum.*

The factory initially was designed to process 350 tons of beets per day and was upgraded to 400 tons a day in 1899. At the time of that upgrade, much of the original processing machinery was replaced with newer and more efficient equipment. The factory was originally designed to burn oil, but that too was changed in the upgrade to coal, as the lower price of coal had made it a more desirable fuel.

Research indicates that, over this factory's short lifespan, the supply of beets was a constant problem. "The sugar factory campaign is expected to close in about a week. The beets originally grown for the factory [Norfolk] were exhausted some weeks ago and the plant has since been running on beets raised for the Ames factory."[6]

This example of shortage of beets for processing should have been a warning for the town, the growers and the factory that all was not good with the future of the factory. It does seem strange that at the same time they were running short on beet supply, they were spending $35,000 (roughly $1,000,000 in today's dollars) on improvements. One of the reasons for the lack of beets is that many of the farmers decided that other crops, especially corn, could be more profitable, as they required considerably less hand labor. Sugar beets at the turn of the last century were very labor intensive and therefore more expensive for the farmer to grow, despite the rate of return on the crop. As fewer acres of beets were grown near the factory, the viability of its operation decreased. As late as October 1904, the plant

Streetcar no. 80 from Norfolk to the Sugar Factory, 1891. *Cora Beets Collection courtesy Elkhorn Valley Museum.*

manager was touting the success of that year's campaign. "Work at the sugar factory, during the first week of the fall campaign, has started in very satisfactory way and manager Bundick anticipates one of the best runs that has ever been known in Norfolk."[7]

Over the next few weeks, it must have come as quite a shock to everyone concerned when it was announced that the factory was closing at the end of the campaign! An editorial in the *Omaha Bee* stated:

> *The removal of the beet sugar factory from Norfolk is explained upon the grounds that the neighboring farmers find other crops more profitable than growing beets for the sugar factory.*[8]

In addition, the *Norfolk News* stated:

> *It is not at all improbable that the machinery of the sugar factory will soon be removed from the plant at this place to Lamar, Col., where a new plant will be erected.*[9]

> *The reason for removing the factories machinery is given by the American Beet Sugar Company to be an insufficient acreage of beets in the territory contiguous to the factory here, to warrant further operating of the factory.*[10]

The sugar company wasted no time in removing the machinery from the plant, as a news article the next January stated. "Fifty Car Loads Gone…. Just as an even half hundred carloads of sugar factory machinery have been shipped out of the Norfolk plant to the new location at Lamar, Col."[11]

Shortly thereafter, the community was left with an empty factory and a lack of other types of companies interested in locating in it. The sweet dreams of the community had been smashed, the investment they had made was gone and they were left with very little. This pattern would soon be repeated at the next factory built in Nebraska, at Ames.

AMES

The third sugar factory in Nebraska was built by another group with outside financing in 1899.

> *The Ames factory will be built by a new corporation which has been organized through the efforts of the men behind the Standard Cattle and Feeding Company who have secured the co-operation and support of a number of wealthy Boston capitalists. The Oxnard Construction company of New York has been given the contracts for the construction and installation which provide for the erection of a plant with a capacity of 1,000 tons per day. For the present the machinery put in will have the capacity of only 500 tons per day, but everything will be so arranged that it can be doubled within a year or two.[12]*

The tiny town of Ames became a boomtown almost overnight. As factory construction progressed, new homes were being built for the factory workers and their families. Both the Union Pacific and the Elkhorn Railroads built track to the factory site from opposite directions.

> *The new factory, which will have double the capacity of either the Grand Island or Norfolk factories, is situated two miles north and a half mile west of Ames, west of the place known as the Mills farm.[13]*

> *The buildings except for a few of the smaller ones, will be entirely fireproof, no wood being used in their construction, the floors being of concrete and the framework of steel and walls of brick. The plan of*

Sugar Factory at Ames, Nebraska, circa 1900. *Legacy of the Plains Museum Collection, Gering, Nebraska.*

construction is the same as that of the "Skyscrapers," the framework of steel plates and girders being first put up, then the walls, no weight whatever resting on the latter.[14]

This plant was a state-of-the-art facility. The factory was to have a larger production capacity than the Norfolk and Grand Island plants combined and be more efficient and therefore cheaper to operate than either of the other two. The fact that a cattle company might be involved should not come as a surprise, as the byproduct of beet pulp had already been determined to make a very good livestock feed. The factory went into operation for the next beet harvest in the fall of 1899.

Operations continued for several years, with the area harvest sometimes being partially redirected to the Norfolk plant, which had run out of beets. That changed after the closure of the Norfolk plant at the end of 1904. Some of the farmers in the Norfolk area wanted to continue to grow beets but no longer had a nearby factory to process them. One of them contacted the Ames factory to inquire if it would be interested in their beets. Part of the necessary conditions for the farmers was that they would weigh the beets at a dump near Norfolk adjacent to one of the railroads to transport the beets to Ames. This would provide a better return to the farmers than having them weighed at the factory, many miles away. The Ames management agreed, if the farmers would contract for at least three hundred acres. It appears that nearly seven hundred acres were contracted for the 1905 crop, so the deal was consummated and beets were shipped from the Norfolk area to the Ames plant. The Ames plant also paid a higher rate per ton than had the last Norfolk contract.

The capacity to process beets was nearly doubled for the 1905 crop in order to absorb the additional beets. The good times for both the farmers and the Ames plant owners did not last long. Through a combination of many things, including leaf spot disease, the Ames plant ceased operations after the 1908 campaign. The plan to move the factories' equipment to another site was detailed in a newspaper in 1909.

> TO MOVE SUGAR FACTORY, Plant at Ames will be transferred to Scottsbluff.…
> Mr. Leavitt said that with the extension of the Interstate ditch the machinery
> in the sugar beet factory at Ames would be transferred to Scotts Bluff, and
> that the North Platte section of Nebraska gave abundant promise of being
> one of the most fertile sections of the United States.[15]

The "abundant promise" mentioned in the article was prophetic and soon realized in the North Platte Valley, as seven factories would be built there in the next twenty years. The Scottsbluff mill would be opened within a year, as the movement and demolition of the Ames plant happened quickly. "Work on dismantling of the sugar factory [at Ames] is progressing rapidly. The brick walls are mostly torn down, leaving the steel frame and inside machinery exposed. It will not be a great while before this old landmark is a thing of the past."[16]

With the exception of the Grand Island mill, the story of the Sugar Beet industry in eastern Nebraska was at its end. No additional plants would be built, although there is much speculation as to the reason why. Omaha newspaper articles at this time repeatedly expressed frustration editorially as to why there was no sugar mill in Omaha. The press blamed the commercial club (predecessor of the chamber of commerce) for not trying harder to recruit a mill for Omaha. They were especially upset when tiny Ames got a mill not too far from Omaha when they had none.

Another location that never got a mill was North Platte. It would seem that the city would be in an ideal geographic position for a factory, but it never happened. The closest it ever got was in 1905–6, when Howard Leavitt, owner of the Ames plant, met with the North Platte Commercial

Club. Leavitt asked for assurances for a needed amount of acres of beets, and the commercial club made verbal commitments that I can only assume were never met. The factory was never built, and I can find nothing further about the proposal. The future of the Sugar Beet industry in Nebraska and eastern Wyoming was in the North Platte Valley in Morrill, Scotts Bluff and Goshen Counties, not in the east.

4

SUGAR VALLEY

A t about this same time, experimental growing of sugar beets in the North Platte Valley had shown some promise. That growing promise was supplemented with an extensive irrigation system that was being developed in the western end of the North Platte Valley, the arrival of the Chicago, Burlington and Quincy Railroad (CB&Q) on the north side of the North Platte River in about 1900 and the arrival of the Union Pacific (UP) on the south side in 1911. These factors, combined with the much dryer climate on the high plains, made the North Platte Valley an ideal place to grow and process sugar beets.

Sugar beets had been grown in the Scottsbluff area for a few years before a factory was built there. The first commercial raising of beets was apparently by Otto Jurgens. His beets, when harvested, were shipped by rail to the plant in Ames. By 1908, Great Western Sugar Company contracted for 1,500 acres of beets in the valley. These were also shipped by rail this time to the GW plant in Sterling, Colorado.

The factory at Scottsbluff was the first one constructed in the valley. Although most information in print states that the building materials as well as the machinery for the factory were obtained from the defunct Ames factory, at least one report, published in the *Sugar Press* in an article by William Maupin of the *Gering Midwest* newspaper, contradicts that. The article states, "The machinery of the Norfolk factory was purchased, which together with considerable new machinery went into the erection of the Scottsbluff plant in 1910."[17]

Regardless of which is correct (and there is conclusive evidence in research material that supports the Ames plant), the factory at Scottsbluff was built and commenced operations in the fall of 1910. It is the only one of the seven plants in this book that will still be in operation for the 2019–20 campaign. Factories were constructed and operated by Great Western in Gering in 1916, Bayard in 1917, Mitchell in 1918, Minatare (started in 1920 but construction was suspended and finally completed in 1926) and Lyman in 1920. A factory in Torrington, Wyoming, was built by the Holly Sugar Company and began operation in 1926.

The story of the sugar beet industry in the North Platte Valley is a significant part of the history of the valley in the first half of the twentieth century. The construction of the factories, the raising of the crop, the development of the irrigation system, the construction of the CB&Q, the UP and the North Platte Valley Railway, as well as the arrival of immigrant and seasonal labor all play a significant role in this story. A great deal of additional detail on most of those subjects, as well as many photographs, some of which have never been published before, will make up the story of this book. Let's begin the journey!

5

THE FACTORIES

SCOTTSBLUFF, NEBRASKA

The Great Western Sugar Company had already built several factories in northern Colorado by the early part of the twentieth century. Factories were already operating, or soon to open, in Loveland, Greeley, Eaton and Windsor. Construction and operation of the Great Western Railroad from Loveland had also begun. This sugar beet activity in Colorado and eastern Nebraska did not go unnoticed by folks in the North Platte Valley.

In 1902, Otto Jurgens, a local proponent of growing sugar beets in the North Platte Valley, met with H.G. Leavitt, then president of the Standard Beet Sugar Company of Ames, Nebraska. As previously mentioned, Jurgens had grown some beets in the previous few seasons and proposed that Leavitt consider a factory in the Scottsbluff area. Jurgens sent a sample of his beets to Leavitt, who was impressed with their quality. In 1905, Jurgens and A.J. Bailey, field man for the Standard Company, convinced a few skeptical local farmers that beets could be grown in the valley. A total of 160 acres were contracted for, which was a sufficient quantity for a test of the practicality of growing beets on a commercial scale in the valley. In the 1906 season, farmers were less skeptical based on the successful growing in the previous season, and 450 acres were contracted for. Much of that crop was lost to a terrible sandstorm on June 8. Overall, the experiment was still deemed successful. Getting the beets to the factory in Ames was a problem, as there were no facilities in the area designed for beet loading to railcars.

The loading of beets at the stations was some job as there was no regular equipment or no dumps as there are today. We had to use all sorts of makeshifts. All kinds of cars were loaded, stock cars, refrigerator cars, box cars, in fact anything that would run on rails. Stock cars were considered easy to load because six teams would crowd around one car, a board was knocked off the sides, and the beets were shoveled through this opening, a team on each end and two teams on each side. The meanest cars to load were the box cars, as in shoveling into the small pigeonholes at the ends, about half the beets fell back on to the shoveler, causing a great loss of temper. Shoveling into piles nowadays cannot be compared with the aggravating work of loading cars in the early days. No beets were piled and many days there were no cars. Consequently a grower often had to make several trips to get his wagon back.[18]

At the end of the 1906 season, everything looked good for the future of beet growing in the valley when the Standard Beet Sugar Company of Ames financially collapsed and went into receivership. As land under irrigation in the valley increased with the completion of the Tri-State and Government ditches, the promise of successful growing of a crop like sugar beets increased. "In 1908 the Great Western Sugar Company came into the valley and obtained 1500 acres. The beets were shipped to Sterling, Colorado."[19]

In 1909, the assets of the Standard Beet Sugar Company of Ames were acquired by the new Scottsbluff Sugar Company. Much of the building was disassembled and, along with the machinery, moved to Scottsbluff.

The pieces were reassembled at its current site on the east side of Scottsbluff and began operation as the Scottsbluff Sugar Company for the 1910 campaign. There is not perfect clarity as to how the Scottsbluff Sugar Company was absorbed quickly into the Great Western Sugar Company family in 1910. From that time to the present day, although ownership has changed a few times, this factory is the last one to be operating for the 2019 season and beyond.

The factory conducted its first campaign in the fall of 1910. The amount of sugar beets it could process in the first year was about 1,200 tons per day. It appears that much of that first crop was probably brought directly to the factory by wagon. Movement by rail was critical to provide sufficient volume

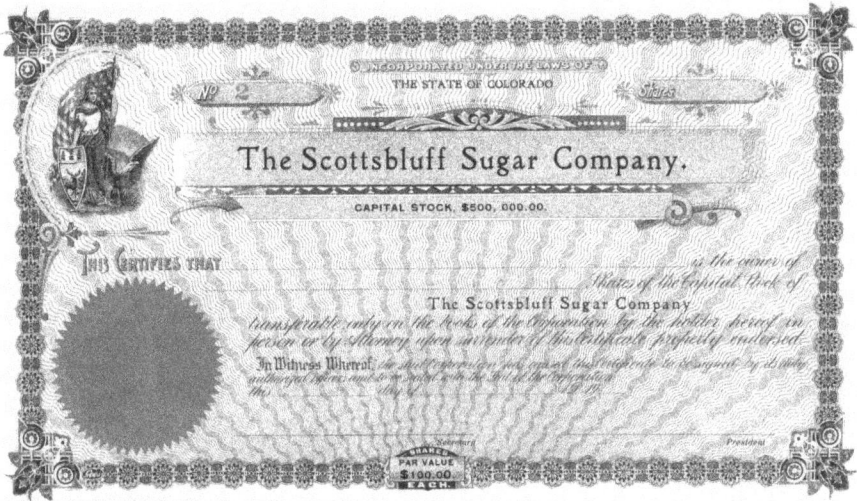

Scottsbluff Sugar Company stock certificate. *Zemank collection, Legacy of the Plains Museum, Gering, Nebraska.*

Scottsbluff Sugar Company office, circa 1910. Star-Herald *photo.*

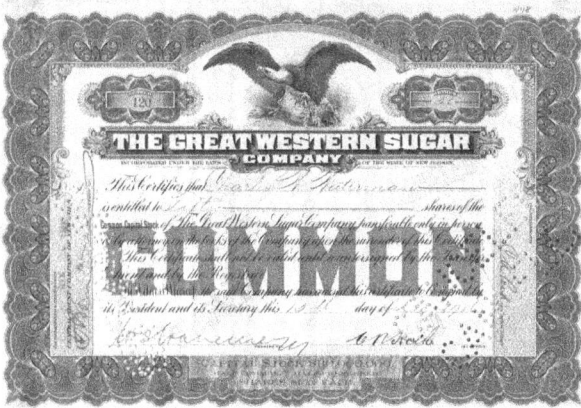

Left: Great Western stock certificate, 1906. *Legacy of the Plains Museum Collection, Gering, Nebraska.*

Below: Scottsbluff Sugar Factory under construction, 1910. *Legacy of the Plains Museum Collection, Gering, Nebraska.*

of beet availability to process and was implemented as soon as possible from a limited number of beet dumps primarily on the Burlington main line through the valley. (Beet receiving stations were called "dumps" then and are called "receiving stations" now.)

Within a few years, the plant was operating at maximum efficiency and was one of the production leaders for Great Western.

As World War I began, demand for American sugar increased dramatically, as production in Europe had all but ceased because of the war. The United States supplied a significant portion of the sugar that could reach Europe, much of it from beets, which led to expanded planting of acres of beets. This in turn taxed the capacity of this existing Scottsbluff factory, leading to the construction of several other GW factories in the valley within a few years. All of these factors in turn created a demand for better railroad availability in closer proximity to the beet fields. Long trips by wagon were inefficient and unreliable, because the crude trails (they probably shouldn't

Top: Scottsbluff beet sheds, 1911. *Legacy of the Plains Museum Collection, Gering, Nebraska.*

Bottom: Wagonloads of beets. *Legacy of the Plains Museum Collection, Gering, Nebraska.*

be called roads at this point) would become instant quagmires after a heavy rain or early snowstorm during the harvest. This meant in many cases that the factory might run out of beets for a short time, creating problems for labor and management.

The railroad situation was soon addressed on the north side of the river with the construction of several "beet spurs" by the Burlington Railroad for Great Western in 1920–21. This will be covered in greater detail in a later chapter. An early beet dump on the main line about

Top: Scottsbluff Sugar Factory in operation, circa 1912. *Postcard from Jack Schmidt collection.*

Bottom: Scottsbluff dump panorama, 1923. *Mike Zeiler family photo.*

three miles west of the factory was constructed in 1909, about where Twentieth Street and Avenue I intersect today. This dump operated until it was dismantled in 1933.

With the construction of additional factories at Gering (1916), Bayard (1917) and Mitchell (1920), the production capacity to meet the world's (and the nation's) demand for sugar may have been more than met, at least for the short term. As Europe started to rebuild after the devastation of the Great War, the production of sugar from sugar beets slowly resumed on the continent. This, in turn with increased production, flat demand and inconsistent tariff policies, resulted in falling prices. Great Western struggled for a few years. Factory construction at another plant in Minatare was suspended for several years, and no other GW plant would be built in

Above: Scottsbluff factory in operation, circa 1920. Scottsbluff Star-Herald.

Left: Scottsbluff factory, circa 1950. *Colorado State University, Agricultural and Natural Resources Archive, Archives and Special Collections.*

the valley until Minatare was finally completed in 1926 and Lyman in 1927. The building boom was over at that point.

Over the next sixty years, there were many changes in the sugar beet industry and at the Scottsbluff factory. One thing that was determined fairly early on was that cattle and sheep love beet pulp, a byproduct of the sugar-making process. And it was a healthy feed for them. After the sugar is extracted from the beet, the pulp that remains has a fairly high nutritional value and therefore is a logical added benefit to the sugar company. By 1924, a feedlot had been established on the east side of the Scottsbluff factory. "The Scottsbluff company feeding operations began on May 5 [1924], when 521 head of cattle were placed on pasture followed by 432 more head on May 21. They were brought in during October with a gain in weight of

Sheep feeding at the Scottsbluff factory, 1920s. Sugar Press *magazine*.

Aerial view of Scottsbluff factory, circa 1960. Feedlots are on the left. *Colorado State University, Agricultural and Natural Resources Archive, Archives and Special Collections.*

302 pounds per head. We are now feeding 1,200 ewes, 7,100 lambs, 1,179 steers, 83 cows and 63 calves."[20]

In 1959, the factory received two proposals for expansion of the feedlots to either a cattle capacity of 2,960 or an even larger one with a capacity of 3,439. In the information I have found, I have been unable to determine if either proposal was adopted and built.

By the 1924 campaign, the Scottsbluff factory had increased the amount of beets it sliced in a day to a maximum of "2,533 tons"[21] from the first year, 1910, to a maximum of 1,200 tons. Sugar for many years at the factories was packaged in 100-pound bags, stored and then shipped out to markets, usually by rail in boxcars. According to company records, in 1945, Scottsbluff had the ability to store 330,000 bags of sugar at one time. In later years, bulk sugar was stored in huge silos. This was a benefit to the company, but it also presented new dangers that would affect this factory as well as Bayard in the future.

Housing the Workers

One of the problems discovered early on was the fact that there was insufficient housing available for the large influx of workers required to first build, and then operate, the factory. By 1916, the situation had become so acute that Great Western itself decided to build housing for employees to keep them working there longer.

> *During the past year the Great Western Sugar Company has experienced such difficulty in getting and keeping its employees at the company's various factories, that from time to time much attention has been focused upon the industrial housing problem, and this year saw the commencement of buildings for the proper housing of the company's employees, especially during the campaign season. The problem was carefully worked out so as to meet the requirements of the individual employee. Some of the employees are single men, some married and with children, so it was necessary to build several types of houses to meet the different requirements.*[22]

The company chose to address the situation with construction of several types of lodging at six locations that existed in 1916. Scottsbluff was the only one addressed in Nebraska at the time. The largest of the housing choices was a dormitory for single men constructed of high-quality brick at 1413 East Overland. A common plan, with a few apparent variations, was used for the dorms in Scottsbluff and five locations in Colorado. As can been seen in the accompanying drawing for the dorm, it appears that the actual building constructed in Scottsbluff was a mirror image of the initial plan. Note that the peaked entrance and the location of the second-floor dormer is flipped from the drawing to what is shown in the photo of the recently remodeled dorm as it appears in April 2019. The dorm was 147 feet long, 31½ feet wide and two stories tall and designed to house seventy men. A kitchen and dining area was included on the first floor. The dorms were designed for two men per room, and there were modern washrooms with showers and toilets on each floor. The buildings are equipped with electricity and steam boilers in the basement for heat.

In addition, an unknown number of two-room apartment houses and five-room, four-room and three-room houses were also built at undetermined locations. The record does not show how many, if any, were built in Scottsbluff at that time. Reliable information suggests that some of this other housing was built there at a later date.

Scottsbluff dormitory as it appeared in April 2019. *Photo by the author.*

Drawing of proposed Scottsbluff GW dormitory, 1916. Sugar Press *magazine*.

Great Western had to deal with this same type of housing shortage in most of the Nebraska facilities, and most of the factories built in the valley had some type of GW housing constructed nearby. Unlike many large companies today, Great Western Sugar recognized a problem, and rather than just complain about it, it took action, at its own expense, to solve it.

The Sugar Beet Demonstration Trains

In the mid-1920s, Great Western Sugar approached both the Burlington and the Union Pacific Railroads to help provide educational resources to help the growers increase their knowledge of growing beets. The belief was that this should increase the quantity of beets grown and the sugar content and generate more traffic for the railroads. At that time, both railroads had agricultural departments that were intended to do just that. By improving the growing practices of the farmers, the railroads would benefit with increased freight traffic. The idea of running special trains, dubbed the "Big Beet Specials,"[23] was arrived at as a way to take the information to the growers, rather than making them come to some educational facility. The first trains ran in 1925. These trains were operated by both railroads in Nebraska, Wyoming and Colorado for three years, finally ending after 1927. Union Pacific ran the trains as special trains, and the Burlington attached them to regularly scheduled trains to move them from town to town.

Newspaper ad for Beet Demonstration Train. Gering Courier, *March 18, 1927.*

The purpose of the initial and later trains was to feature "Speakers and Special Exhibit Designed to Further Movement for 'Another ton of Beets per Acre.'"[24] The success of the improved production by implementing the improved practices would increase the annual beet payment in the valley by about half a million dollars.

> *Beet Demonstration Trains Attract Big Attendances Monday. At both Gering and Scottsbluff, the sugar beet demonstration trains drew much larger attendances than was expected by those who are fostering the sentiment and plans to secure at least another ton of beets per acre for 1925. Reports are that at other points in the valley similarly good attendance was on hand.*[25]

In April 1926 and March 1927, similar trains were operated. "It requires little or no more land—the same acre, the same tools and the same effort will be used in making 14-ton, or even 16-ton average yield, as is used in making lower yields."[26] The plan was successful. "As a result of this activity, the average yield of the beet crop in our territory in 1926 was 15.19 tons per acre, as compared with 11.8 tons per as ten-year average yield."[27] (This increase included the Colorado, Wyoming and Nebraska areas.) The operation was an obvious success but apparently was discontinued after 1927. At least in part this may have been a result of good crop prices in 1926 and 1927 and a return to lower average prices in 1928.

Disputes between Growers and Great Western Sugar

Despite a still growing industry in the mid-1920s, cracks in the unity between company and growers were appearing in the North Platte Valley. In an ad in the *Gering Courier* on November 20, 1925, the sugar company disputes reports that it deems "propaganda"[28] regarding a report circulated among growers claiming to be from the sugar company that apparently hints at major changes in the way the sugar crop would be paid for beginning in 1925. A resolution from the Beet Growers Association of Nebraska was reported to have been adopted by the Great Western Board of Directors. This is refuted in the *Courier* ad.

The ad goes on to say that the sugar company is trying to raise the payments by selling the sugar produced in an area that will accept the higher prices the company is trying to get for its finished product. This dispute is far from over; the second ad from the *Courier* from February 24, 1928, reneges on

A Frank Statement
To the Valley Public on the Sugar Company's Price Policy

When given the facts the public's sense of fairness can be relied upon to protect itself against propaganda.

By price allowances the Company is increasing the proportion of its sales in high yielding territory. The Company again assures the people of the Valley that these allowances to the trade do not decrease the price paid for beets. On the contrary, increased sales in high price markets insure a higher payment for beets than the growers otherwise would realize.

Growers will be paid in the regular way on the net price as if no special allowance had been made.

Officers of The Mountain States Beet Grower's Marketing association of Colorado have endorsed the company's present selling policy and offered to cooperate in furthering the program and thus aiding their members.

MORE LIGHT ON THE LOCAL RESOLUTIONS

The resolution sent to the valley newspapers last week as coming from the Beet Growers Association of Nebraska, before released for publication, were NOT adopted at any meeting of the Board.

A majority of the directors had never heard of the resolutions.

Subsequent endorsement can not alter those facts. Company representatives sought in meetings with individual directors to explain the true conditions. Before Tuesday's meeting of a quorum of the Board, company representatives asked permission to meet in session with the Directors. This permission was denied the Great Western although representatives of another company were admitted.

That an impartial consideration of the Great Western's price policy can not be obtained from the Board of Directors is a logical conclusion in view of the Board's position.

The false implications or charges contained in the resolutions are: That our growers "are being made victims" of the company's sales policy; that the company would lower the net price to warrant no more than $6 per ton of beets; that our policy is "dictated by cane sugar interests;" that it is "an attempt to frighten or punish growers;" or that the price policy reduces the payment for beets by this company.

Such implied or direct charges the Great Western Sugar Company specifically and totally denies.

No criticism of the Association as an organization is intended in this statement. The company believes that the directors who have taken this action are ill-advised and incorrectly informed.

OUR SALES POLICY AND DIFFERENCES IN BEET PAYMENTS

The resolutions mentioned a difference in beet payments in the Valley. Wrong conclusions have been drawn on this subject. Clear to every one should be the reasons for the differences in the price paid per ton of beets on sliding scale contracts. The facts are presented in the following table:

COMPARISON OF BEET PAYMENTS AND SLIDING SCALE CONTRACTS

Company	Net Per Bag of Sugar	Sugar Content	Paid Per Ton Beets	Contract Price of Beets Basis	Contract Right to Pay
Great Western					
(Colorado-Nebraska)	$5.559	16.46%	$7.50	$7.35	—
(Billings-Lovell)	$5.897	17.29%	$8.17	$8.17	—
Holly					
(Western Slope of Colorado)	$6.034	16.75%	$7.613	$8.32	7½ cts
(Torrington)	$6.011	16.91%	$8.40	$8.40	Same
American Beet					
(Grand Island)	$6.59	15.76%	$8.086	$8.58	50 cts

The lower Great Western payment per ton of beets in the valley was due mainly to our lower net price per bag on a larger output. Our present sales policy will establish a preference for Great Western Sugar in the higher price territories. The same object is being pursued in our advertising campaign there and in personal contact work among the trade.

With a sliding scale contract as high as any offered growers in the Valley, the net price of sugar used as a basis of payment for beets will be increased by our present sales policy. Increased sales where the effect will be to increase his beet payment deserves the support of every Great Western Beet raiser.

The Great Western Sugar Company

GW newspaper ad regarding the grower/factory contract dispute. *Gering Courier, November 20, 1925.*

A Statement on The Beet Contract

By the Great Western Sugar Company

February 21, 1928

During the recent conferences on the 1928 beet contract, notwithstanding substantial progress toward a closer relationship between the cooperative associations and the sugar company and despite sincere efforts to reach an agreement, differences of opinion developed over the beet price. The company therefore feels that farmers and public at large are entitled to a statement of its position.

Conditions in Sugar Industry

It is regrettable that conditions do not justify the company's continuing the high minimum guarantee made in 1926 and 1927. Sugar from the 1928 beet crop will not be produced until next autumn and the bulk of the crop will not be sold until the year 1929. To forecast the market accurately during that distant period is obviously impossible, particularly since the situation is complicated by artificial restriction policies surrounding sugar production in foreign countries.

In the last two seasons Great Western growers enjoyed the highest guaranteed minimum payment for beets in the United States. Expectations of sugar content and net price on which the guarantee was based did not materialize. As a result the company's earnings have fallen below what is necessary to attract and keep capital in the business, to provide for expansion, and to continue the high character of service the company desires to provide. Maintenance of a sound financial condition and an adequate rate of income over a period of years are essential to payment of an attractive price to the farmer.

By reason of the high guaranteed payment of the last two seasons and an unusually low level of sugar prices the sliding scale embodied in the 1926 and 1927 contracts has not up to the present justified payments in excess of the $8.00 guarantee. When that scale was formulated in 1924 it provided for a division of the proceeds based upon the company's operating results for the previous ten year period. In adopting the scale the company then stated that later improvements in technical performance would be shared with growers. In the intervening four campaigns factory efficiency has been improved and this is reflected in the new sliding scale now offered.

The 1928 Beet Contract

The sliding scale has been increased in the 1928 beet contract, and the bonus for volume of sugar production has been retained. At sugar content and price levels likely to apply, the new scale is 33 to 58 cents per ton higher than the 1927 scale. Under no conditions will the contract pay less than $7.00 and it embodies participating features for the growers better than ever before offered.

Based on the company's present extraction the new sliding scale gives the full equivalent of the "50-50" demand so often made in previous negotiations. With the bonus for volume the contract pays more than half of the sugar value, ranging up to fifty-four per cent. The production of a volume of beets sufficient to insure the application of the bonus is a factor which is vary largely in the control of the growers themselves, and is easily attainable. Production in each of the three districts in the past season exceeded the quantity stipulated for the application of the full 50 cents per ton bonus.

To say that this contract will not pay more than the $7.00 guarantee is to assume the most pessimistic view of the four controlling factors,—harvested acreage, yield per acre, sugar content, and price. While there is uncertainty as to any single one of these factors it is difficult to believe that they will all result unfavorably.

Better Understanding Reached on Some Issues

Reduction of the initial payment removed the necessity of a clause relating to lowering of the sugar tariff, and this provision was eliminated for 1928.

The report of a joint committee of the conference which prepared instructions for taking tare will be followed by the company. Appointment of check taremen to represent the growers has always been agreeable to the company as evidenced by provision therefor in past contracts. We feel that the employment of such taremen will remove many causes of misunderstanding.

Sentiment in the conferences was markedly in favor of restricting piling of beets until after October 15, to increase sugar content and tonnage and to reduce the large mutual loss of sugar occasioned by too rapid a rate of delivery in the harvest.

The company feels confident that with a little study of the new contract the growers will realize its unusual attractiveness, and that a large acreage will be grown. During the conference the company offered its most favorable terms, and any contract which provides for a higher basis of payment can not be accepted.

The Great Western Sugar Company

Another newspaper ad regarding the grower/factory contract dispute placed by Great Western Sugar Company. Gering Courier, *February 24, 1928.*

the higher minimum guaranteed payment promised for 1926 and 1927 and cites the changing conditions in the market for sugar, at least in part related to tariff policies and the "artificial restriction policies surrounding sugar production in foreign countries."[29] Because of these restrictions, predicting the price that sugar will sell for on the open market, therefore affecting the amount the company can pay for the beets, is very complicated.

> In the last two seasons Great Western growers enjoyed the highest guaranteed minimum payment for beets in the United States. Expectation of sugar content and the net price on which the guarantee was based on did not materialize. As a result the company's earnings have fallen below what is necessary to attract and keep capital in the business, to provide for expansion, and to continue the high character of service the company desires to provide. Maintenance of a sound financial condition and an adequate rate of income over a period of years is essential to payment of an attractive price to the farmer.[30]

As with anyone, the beet farmers were not happy about the possible cut in what they were to be paid for their crop. The combination of inconsistent tariff policies by the United States and other nations, a U.S. sugar subsidy at times and not others, boom-and-bust world demand for sugar and the eventual replacement of much of the demand for sugar with other sweeteners eventually led to the situation the industry experiences today: a much smaller market and a severe reduction in the need for many sugar beet factories in both the North Platte Valley and the nation.

Handling the Finished Sugar Product

Traditionally, processed beet sugar was packaged in one-hundred-pound burlap bags that, when filled, were then stacked in the large warehouse space that was found at each of the valley's factories. A large part of the bagged sugar was then loaded into boxcars and shipped out of the area to the markets as it was needed. This procedure required large storage areas, thousands of bags and a considerable amount of hand labor moving, stacking and then unstacking the piles to load them into boxcars. There was also a considerable amount of potential for accidents, as stacks of one-hundred-pound bags, thirty or more bags high, presented a formidable risk of injury in the loading and unloading process.

Stacks of one-hundred-pound sacks of sugar at the Mitchell factory, circa 1930. *Joan Johns and Karen Jackson family photo.*

In an article of the spring 1946 *Sugar Press* magazine, L.J. Welsh makes the case against continuing to package into one-hundred-pound sacks. The bulk of the demand is for sugar in variously sized packages, and that makes the old way obsolete.

> *Instead of one* [one-hundred-pound] *burlap package of the early 1920's, your company is sending GW Pure Sugar out to its trade today in sizes and types requiring sixteen different packages. It is fair to estimate that within two more years this figure will go over the twenty mark....It is impossible to forecast distribution for a year in advance. As an example, witness the effects of the rationing program* [during World War II] *which have boosted 5-pound packages from an insignificant 3% prior to the war to approximately 20% at present. It is a terrific waste to put up sugar during the campaign in 100-pound bags and then pour it out in the following summer to make small packages. The advantages of bin storage becomes evident in the light of these conditions.*[31]

The article goes on to cite additional reasons for bin storage, including increased storage capacity, the savings on labor and reduced loss by not packaging the old way. It also emphasizes the ability to order smaller bags as needed, thus reducing inventory bag costs. In addition, packaging can be done as needed over the year rather than all at once during the harvest processing, and shipping a better marketable product is achieved when the bags are filled as needed and not stored after filling. The 1946 article mentions that storage silos were being built or planned for the near future at six Great Western factories, including Scottsbluff.

The first four sugar bins (silos) at Scottsbluff were built in the late 1940s; a second group of four taller bins were built adjacent to the original four around 1960. These eight bins gave the Scottsbluff factory significantly more storage capacity than any of the other Great Western factories in the North Platte Valley.

One of the things not apparently given serious consideration at the time was the explosiveness of sugar dust. This danger showed itself on the evening of July 20, 1996. A spark, probably caused by a lightning strike, caused all eight bins to be destroyed in a massive explosion. The explosion happened at exactly 10:15 p.m. MDT, according to the stopped clock in the laboratory.

The wreckage of all eight Scottsbluff Bins after the explosion of July 20, 1996. *Rick Myers Photo, Scottsbluff Star-Herald.*

Scottsbluff factory, 1962. *Colorado State University, Agricultural and Natural Resources Archive, Archives and Special Collections.*

Damages exceeded $10 million, and there were a number of injuries and 1 fatality, Gene Juergens, at the factory. Had this happened during the day, when a full summer crew of about 240 workers would have been present, rather than an overnight skeleton crew of about 18, the human carnage would have been much worse. A similar explosion had taken place at the Bayard factory several years earlier. New bins, which hold about 50 percent more sugar, were built soon after but in a different configuration (a straight line of four large silos to the east of the main site instead of two groups of four bins in a square cluster). The foundation and subterranean portion of the four taller old bins was salvaged and used as a foundation for a unique new office for the factory when rebuilt.

The factory has gone through many changes in both site plan and building layout over the 110 years it has operated. The accompanying site map shows the factory land layout in 1923, including the buildings, the feedlots and the railroad configuration at that time. Much has changed over the years. In the beginning, much of the crop came to the factory

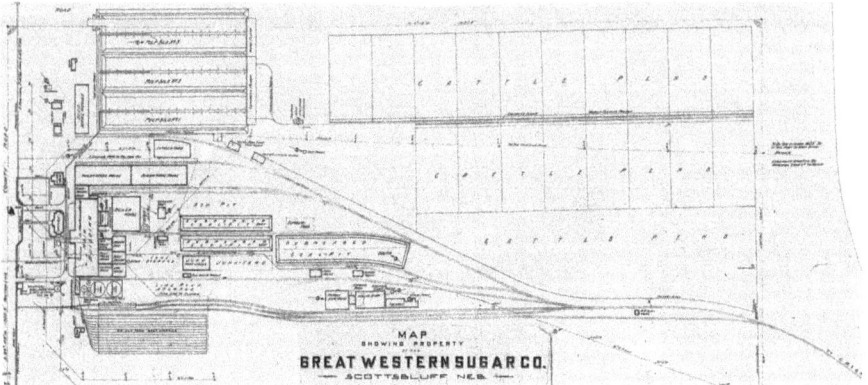

Scottsbluff factory site map, March 3, 1919. *Courtesy Western Sugar Co-op.*

directly by wagon. With the cooperation of the Burlington Railroad, most of the crop was coming to Scottsbluff by rail by 1923 from main-line dumps and from the beet spurs of the North Platte Valley Railway. We'll detail more of those operations in a later chapter.

GERING, NEBRASKA

The next factory built by Great Western in the valley was the factory at Gering. In late 1915, the Great Western Sugar Company announced that beet production in the valley had reached a point where the Scottsbluff factory alone could not process the entire crop in a timely manner. The company announced that a new factory in Gering, just a few miles to the south across the North Platte River, would be the site of that factory. Construction began almost immediately. The Gering factory was the first Great Western plant designed from the ground up by its own engineers. It was the first GW plant considered to be one of the "19 Houses."[32] The "19 Houses" were designed to process beets with high sugar content, 19 percent or more.

Working seven days a week, the construction crew of about five hundred men completed the factory by August 1916, an amazing task in about ten months. The first sugar campaign began in early November 1916. The factory was originally designed to process 1,300 tons of sugar per day, and the first year was very successful. Gering, like the Scottsbluff factory earlier, had problems with labor shortages and housing for the laborers when they

Gering sugar factory construction, March 25, 1916. *Legacy of the Plains Museum Collection, Gering, Nebraska.*

Gering sugar factory construction, June 23, 1916. *Legacy of the Plains Museum Collection, Gering, Nebraska.*

Gering GW dormitory in use in the 1960s as a nursing student dorm for West Nebraska General Hospital as Nelson-Ladely Hall. *Courtesy of Regional West Medical Center.*

were found. A U-shaped brick dormitory of a different, but similar, design was built in Gering in 1917 at Charles Street (Eighth Street today) and Walnut Street (P Street). This U-shaped layout would also be used later in Mitchell, Minatare and Bayard. This facility was later sold to West Nebraska General Hospital in the 1960s, serving as the Nelson-Ladely Hall dormitory for nursing students from about 1966 until 1969. It was torn down in the early 1970s.

Additional housing was also built within the community in short order to meet the exploding demand. The arrival of the Union Pacific in 1911 and the construction of the factory reignited growth in Gering after several years of stagnation while Scottsbluff had grown. The sugar industry was a godsend to grower, worker, businessman and government official alike. It was probably best summed up by the cashier at the Gering factory in June 1929 in a speech to the Gering Chamber of Commerce. J.B. Badgley stated:

> *The figures I give are three-year averages for 1927, 1928 and 1929, three years that are fairly representative. The data given includes only the territory adjacent to the city of Gering and a part of the trade territory, which includes the factory site and receiving stations.*

The average contracted beet acreage was 9,389 acres which yielded just over twelve tons per acre; the average price paid to the growers was $7 per ton or $85 per acre. The gross amount received from an acre of sugar beets is $50 higher than that received from an acre of barley or alfalfa. The 9,389 acres of sugar beets grossed $798,065; the same acreage planted to barley or alfalfa would have grossed only $328,615.

The payroll at the factory averaged $246,568 a year, while the payroll of the Union Pacific men hired in addition to the normal crew was $18,150. Adding the three—excess amount paid for beets over barley or alfalfa, factory payroll, and railroad payroll—total $734,168. In round numbers there has been nearly three-quarters of a million dollars paid out that would not have been paid if the sugar industry were not here.[33]

To put those numbers in perspective, adjusted for inflation, the price per ton in 2019 would be $103, or $1,257 per acre. The total gross income from the 9,389 acres of beets would be $11,802,961! These are incredible numbers and show how important this industry was to the community for many years.

The Gering factory was a very efficient one over the years. Great Western factories competed among themselves for the GW Pennant, which was a measure of the efficiency of the plant relating to production and income verses expenses. Gering, not the largest plant by any measure, tied for the pennant with Fort Morgan in 1931–32 and won the pennant outright in 1932–33, 1940–41, 1955–56 and 1960–61. In all those years, the Scottsbluff plant never achieved that award.

Gering's factory was the first GW plant to be equipped with a pulp dryer. The pulp, primarily used as livestock feed, could then be moved more easily to feedlots not directly adjacent to the factory, as was the case in Scottsbluff. This facility was not without some problems. In 1923, a large fire destroyed the pulp warehouse and everything in it as well as a building next to it. Firemen were handicapped in fighting the fire by the fact that the temperature at the time was twenty-five degrees below zero. The sprinkler system in the building looked like it might have a chance to suppress the fire, but it was not to be. Through heroic efforts in horrible conditions, the fire brigade from the factory, with the assistance of the Gering and Scottsbluff Fire Departments, was successful in saving the expensive pulp-dryer plant and its equipment. The pulp warehouse experienced a second fire in 1926.

The Gering plant continued to operate efficiently for many years from its initial campaign in 1916. Something unique happened at the Gering and

Gering Great Western pennant winners. *Legacy of the Plains Museum Collection, Gering, Nebraska.*

Gering factory, circa 1950. *Colorado State University, Agricultural and Natural Resources Archive, Archives and Special Collections.*

Mitchell plants in the spring of 1944 during World War II. The War Food Administration asked ten sugar beet factories in four states to dehydrate a portion of the 1943 potato crop so it would not go to waste. Between April 5 and May 1, Gering (and Mitchell) processed approximately 36,500 tons of potatoes. According to an article in the *Sugar Press*:

> *Approximately 90 percent of the potatoes were grown in the North Platte Valley. "Without a doubt, the majority of these potatoes would have spoiled in the farmers cellars if it had not been for this program."*[34]
>
> *The dried potato slices were to be used for the production of alcohol, feed and mixed feeds.*[35]

Some of the machinery at the two plants required slight modification for the potato drying, but overall, the process was deemed a success, and the War Food Administration was happy with the end results.

P. H. Mc-Master count-ed 111 trucks of spuds lined up at the Gering factory April 20.

Potato trucks at Gering sugar factory. Sugar Press, *April 20, 1944.*

After the war, the sugar industry was changing rapidly. Plants in the North Platte Valley were soon closed (Minatare and Lyman), and the remaining factories were being improved, in part with the installation of the previously mentioned bulk sugar storage bins. Gering received its bins sometime in the 1950s; an exact date can't be found. The bins, sometimes called prairie skyscrapers, have been a distinctive man-made landmark in the valley for over half a century.

As with the Scottsbluff plant and all the others in the valley, the site layout of the factories changed considerably over the years. The accompanying images show site maps of the Gering factory in 1916 as it was originally configured and again in 1947. The most noticeable difference is the disappearance of the flume high lines at the southwest corner of the property and the addition of new track work adjacent and parallel to the main factory road. On that line is located the wet hopper, the domain of the dinky steam locomotives for many years until about the mid-1970s. Here, the beets were dumped directly into a tunnel with a chemical water bath and flushed into the factory via the tunnel. It was this operation that created the conditions that justified the retention of the steam dinkies for so long. There will be more about them in a later chapter. Note that the Gering factory had not yet received its bulk sugar silos in 1947.

Over the years of operation, the areas that provided beets for the various factories changed. A good example of this is found in an article in the *Gering Courier* from January 21, 1927, under the headline "Gering Factory Run

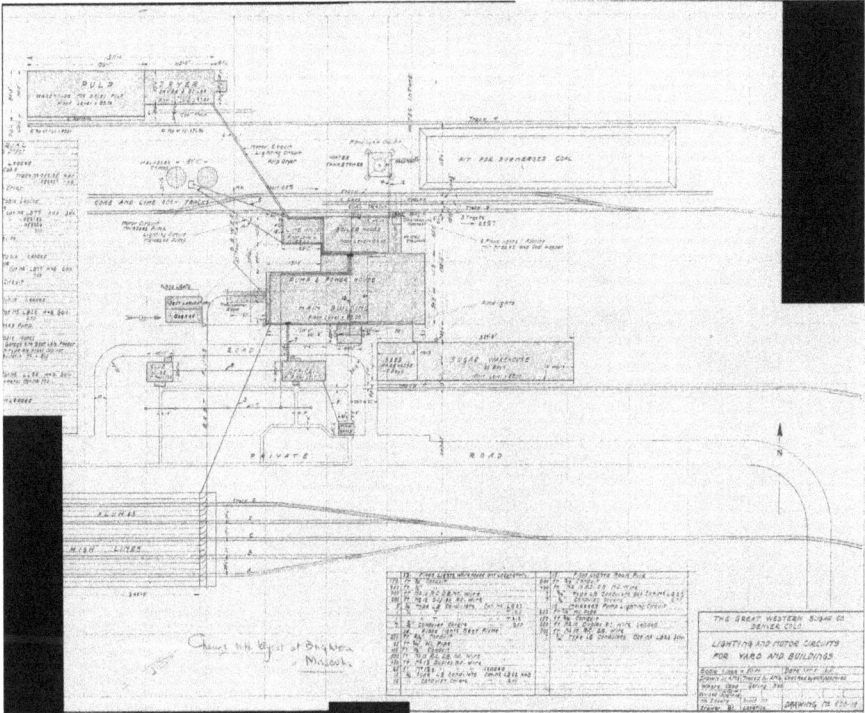

Gering sugar factory site map, 1916. *Courtesy Western Sugar Co-op.*

Ended Last Tuesday."[36] The article explained a decrease in tonnage at the Gering plant:

> *The change in districts* [where the beets would come from] *was occasioned by the building of the Minatare factory, which handled the past year all the beets from the Melbeta and McGrew territory, while beets from Chimney Rock and east of there were slotted to the Bayard factory. Another change gave all beets from Mathison, which is a U.P. Station south of Mitchell, and adjacent territory west of there to the Mitchell plant. The preceding year, all of the beet grown on the south side* [of the North Platte River] *from Wyoming line east as far as O'Fallons, Nebr.* [just west of North Platte] *were handled at the Gering plant. In spite of these changes the Gering factory had the longest run of any in the valley.*[37]

The Gering plant would have considerable increased acreage allotted to it for the next season, as new land in the Gering Valley was to be planted in

Gering Factory looking west toward Scottsbluff National Monument, circa 1960. *Colorado State University, Agricultural and Natural Resources Archive, Archives and Special Collections.*

beets beginning then. There is probably a good reason for this shift, as the new Union Pacific sugar beet spur to the Riford dump in Gering Valley was being built for the 1927 growing season. The 9.8-mile spur south and west from Gering reduced considerably the distance growers in the Gering Valley would have to go to get their crop to the factory. Before this, you needed to be located close to the UP main line through the valley to have easy access to one of the many beet dumps along that line. This probably discouraged a number of potential growers from growing beets in the Gering Valley, simply because it was too far to go to get them to a beet dump and then on to the factory before the spur was built. There will be more about this and the other area beet spurs in a later chapter.

Gering's factory was not immune from accidents. On December 18, 1924, a fire in the sugar warehouse damaged about five thousand one-hundred-pound bags of sugar with an estimated loss of $4,000. The fire started on the top of a stack and may have been smoldering for several days before bursting into flame. Most of the damage was caused when the fire triggered

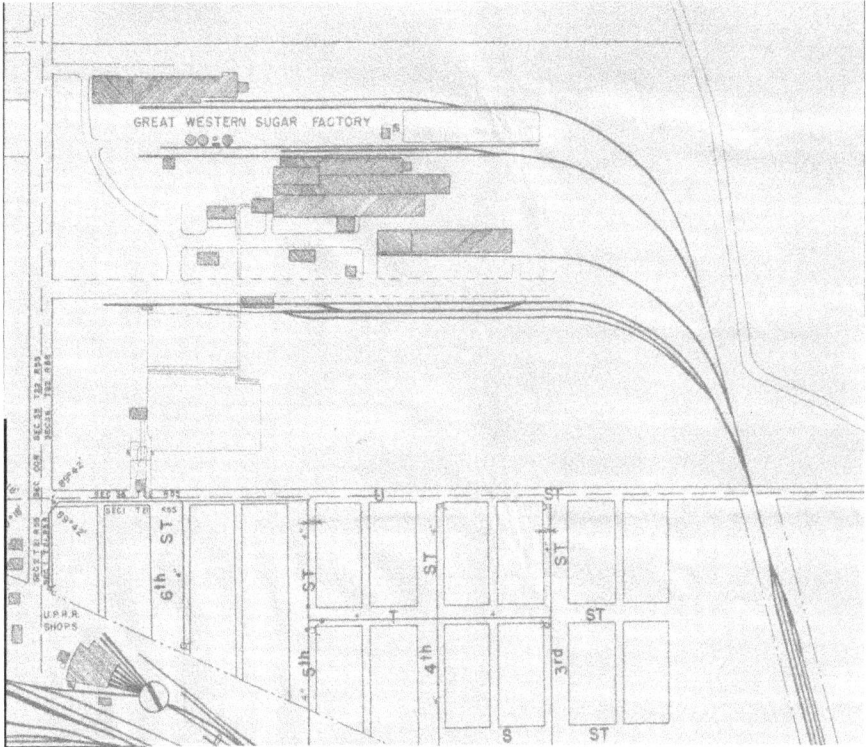

Above: Simplified Gering factory site map, circa 1947. *1947 Gering city map. Author's collection.*

Left: Harvesting beets in the Gering Valley, Dome Rock in the center background, 1960s. *Legacy of the Plains Museum Collection, Gering, Nebraska.*

the automatic sprinkler system, flooding the area with water. It was thought that the wet sugar could be reprocessed through the granulator, and most of it was salvaged and useable.

Although Gering's factory never suffered a catastrophic explosion of its sugar bins, it did have a unique incident on February 15, 1989, when over a million gallons of molasses from a storage tank at the factory ruptured,

Molasses spill at Gering factory, February 15, 1989. Star-Herald *photo by Rick Meyers.*

spilling the substance for a considerable distance on the property. Although the plant was no longer processing beets, sugar and molasses were stored there and some work was still being done in the lab. Three employees were injured by the mess. Total damage was estimated at about $1 million for the tank, several vehicles, a few small buildings and the lost molasses. The event was even commemorated by a local entrepreneur, who produced T-shirts with the inscription "I Survived the Molasses Wave" in Gering, Nebraska. They were a popular item for those looking for something different at the time.

In the years the Gering factory operated, it processed many tons of beets. Beginning with its previously mentioned original capacity of 1,300 tons of beets per day, capacity increased to 1,700 tons and then to 1,950 tons. That number proved to be conservative, as its record for beet slicing for a day hit 2,663 in October 1960.

Although the operation of the Gering factory, along with most all of the others in the valley, is rapidly becoming a distant memory, no one can deny the history-changing events it caused in Gering in the early to mid-twentieth century. Without the factory being built in 1916, Gering would have struggled for survival as many towns in Nebraska and the high plains did. Although Gering was the county seat, one can only speculate if that alone would have been enough to see the city survive and grow. Gering has done better than some of the towns that lost factories as the industry declined, and it strives to continue that survival and growth in the twenty-first century.

BAYARD, NEBRASKA

Construction on the new factory in Bayard began in the fall of 1916 (see photograph below). Located on the west side of town at 804 West Eighth Street, it was built next to the Burlington Railroad main line that ran west up the valley. This was the second factory designed and built by Great Western and the second "19 House" in the valley. Like Gering, it was constructed and in operation in less than one year. As with the Gering factory, Bayard was constructed with a pulp dryer.

The Bayard and Gering factories were originally designed to process 1,300 tons of beets per day. The average tonnage in 1961 was about 1,975 tons per day, and Bayard had a record one-day production of 2,444 tons. This one-day production would have been enough to supply all the sugar needs of the city of Bayard for almost three years!

If you look at the aerial picture on page 60 closely, you can see the Bayard-Everett/Carlson beet spur running from the middle left to the upper right and then curving west across the top of the photo to the northwest. The next photo is a picture of a farmer planting beets in the shadow of Chimney Rock south of Bayard.

According to an article in the May 1922 *Sugar Press*: "The Bayard sugar factory has the distinction of growing and harvesting more than 15,000 acres of sugar beets, producing 164,573 tons and delivered to only six receiving stations. It is safe to say that no other factory in the world produces this tonnage at six receiving stations."[38]

In the circa 1960 aerial picture on the following page, looking north, you can see the original storage bins. If you look closely, you can again also see

Winter construction of Bayard factory, December 1916. Sugar Press *magazine*.

Aerial picture of Bayard factory, looking north, circa 1960. Note beet spur heading north-northwest, ending at the Carlson beet dump. *Colorado State University, Agricultural and Natural Resources Archive, Archives and Special Collections.*

the Bayard-Everett/Carlson beet spur running from the middle left to upper right and then curving west across the top of the photo to the northwest.

The Bayard factory, like its sisters up and down the valley, was not immune to accidents. On September 27, 1923, a disastrous event occurred when a giant flywheel on one of the large engines in the plant exploded. Two employees were injured, one with a broken leg and the other with cuts and bruises. The pieces from the flywheel were propelled for some distance. One large piece weighing a few hundred pounds cut a twelve-inch steam line in two, passed through the roof, flew over the office building and buried itself five feet deep into the lawn! This destruction was expected to stop operation at the mill at least thirty days, delaying the start of the campaign there.

The biggest disaster to strike the Bayard factory came later. Like the mills in Scottsbluff, Gering and Mitchell, it received four bulk storage bins sometime in the 1950s. Like the Scottsbluff factory later, Bayard was the victim of a terrible explosion in the bins on Tuesday May 16, 1972. According to

Tractor planting sugar beets beneath Chimney Rock near Bayard, Nebraska, 1950s. *Colorado State University, Agricultural and Natural Resources Archive, Archives and Special Collections.*

an article in the *Scottsbluff Star-Herald*, "An explosion which rocked most of Bayard at 10:45 a.m. Tuesday did extensive damage, estimated 'in the several hundreds of thousands of dollars' at the Bayard factory of the Great Western Sugar Company."

The blast occurred as employees were unloading bulk sugar from storage silos into railroad cars.

Farmers bring beets directly to the Bayard factory, 1950s. *Colorado State University, Agricultural and Natural Resources Archive, Archives and Special Collections.*

"Cause of the blast which damaged four sugar bins and a warehouse is still under investigation" said Bill L. Phillips, Vice-President in charge of operations for Great Western Sugar Co...." We will rebuild the bulk bins with an estimated construction time of five to six months."...Debris from the bins, each of which are 35 feet in diameter and 180 feet high was scattered over a 300 yard radius. Six vehicles parked behind the factory offices were damaged by large pieces of concrete and steel which fell on them. One pickup truck was totally demolished and a small foreign car received considerable damage.[39]

Although the accident was serious and there were injuries, some serious, to several men at the plant, it was fortunate that no one was killed. The overly optimistic prediction of Mr. Phillips quoted above regarding rebuilding the bins proved to be far from the reality that followed the explosion. For some reason (I would suspect financial), the bins were not replaced for fourteen years. In a February 6, 1986 article in the *Bayard Transcript*, the sugar company received a grant through the City of Bayard for "$493,000 from the Department of Economic Development this week. The monies will be

Aerial picture of Bayard factory, looking north, circa 1970. Note the beet spur heading north-northwest, ending at the Carlson beet dump. *Colorado State University, Agricultural and Natural Resources Archive, Archives and Special Collections.*

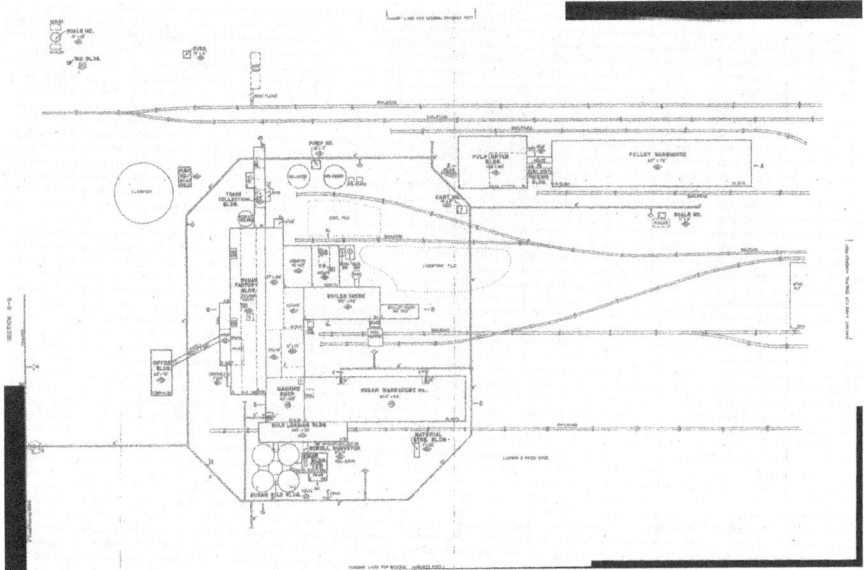

Bayard factory site plan, 1966. *Courtesy Western Sugar Co-op.*

Bayard silo after explosion, May 16, 1972. *Colorado State University, Agricultural and Natural Resources Archive, Archives and Special Collections.*

loaned to Western Sugar Co. to help fund construction of sugar silos at Western Sugars Bayard plant at ten percent interest....Plans for a cluster of four silos will be constructed designed to hold 417,000 hundred weight (of bulk sugar)....Plans for finishing the silos was set for the fall of 1986."[40]

The Bayard factory was a consistent performer. In 1922, it was the highest-ranked Great Western factory in terms of tonnage produced per acre. Again, as in Scottsbluff and Gering before it, Great Western built a dormitory for employees. Like the Scottsbluff facility, it is still in existence today, most recently in the form of a bed-and-breakfast. It currently lies in disrepair, but there is hope in the community that the bed-and-breakfast might reopen in the future.

Bayard dormitory, May 2019. *Photo by the author.*

The Bayard factory was, as were all the sugar factories, a vital part of the economy of that community for about eighty-five years. According to information from Great Western in an undated publication, the company's payroll exceeded $52 for every acre of beets grown as well as many millions of dollars paid to the farmers for their crop. The two beet spurs that served the Bayard factory for many years beginning in 1920 (west) and 1926 (east) will be covered in more detail in a later chapter. The factory and most of its huge economic benefit to Bayard were lost when it closed for beet processing in 2002. The company does contract sugar storage in the bins as of this time.

MITCHELL, NEBRASKA

The story of the Great Western Sugar Factory in Mitchell, Nebraska, appears to have started a decade earlier than the start of actual construction. The Mitchell plant would be the fourth Great Western mill in the Nebraska Panhandle and, like Gering and Bayard before it, would be built by Great Western crews to the standard of the other "19 Houses." According to an article titled "Will We Have a Factory?":[41]

Years ago, before the first factory was built in the North Platte Valley, Mitchell was given what was considered then very favorable considerations as an applicant for the first factory. It was at that time that the Great Western Purchased their Mitchell farm.[42]

The Great Western has owned a farm adjoining Mitchell on the north-west since before they built in Scottsbluff.[43]

The three factories [Scottsbluff, Gering and Bayard] *are over-taxed in handling the beets grown in this valley, and the demand for sugar production is increasing.*[44]

The exact reasons for this initial bypassing of Mitchell are not readily apparent. The Scottsbluff factory (as cited earlier) was not built by Great Western but by the Scottsbluff Sugar Company and then purchased by Great Western. It is possible that when the mill was built at Scottsbluff by another company, the management of Great Western made a strategic decision to protect the valley territory from other companies encroaching on the area by purchasing that mill almost immediately. Why it next built in Gering and Bayard may have been for the same reason. At the time (about 1920), Great Western may have felt more threatened from competition from the east and not from the west. This may have played an important part in the sequence in which the Great Western plants were built. Another quote from the same edition of the *Mitchell Index* states the following:

There are those who believe that Great Western cannot afford longer to leave exposed so favorable a proposition as is offered at Mitchell and so are making haste at this time to close the gap in their territory which might look good to a competing corporation.[45]

We can only say that the general opinion, based on what is known as well as what is surmised, is that sugar will be manufactured in Mitchell before another year rolls around.[46]

The rampant speculation in the previously cited newspaper article was confirmed less than a month later in the December 18, 1919 issue of the *Index*. Again (as is the case most of the time), a story on the front page, "Factory Plans Progressing,"[47] confirms the rumors of a factory to be built in Mitchell starting almost immediately.

All indications point to actual building work in the very near future. Plans for the new sugar factory at Mitchell by the Great Western Sugar Company are unfolding so rapidly one can scarce make note of all surface indications. One peculiar thing about it is that—so far as we are informed—the officials of the company have as yet made no definite details and official statement as to their intentions. Yet the work of preparation goes rapidly forward just the same, and from those in position to know we are informed that but for the severe weather of the past few weeks a large force of men would already be at work.[48]

I can find no specific reference in the *Mitchell Index* to a formal building announcement. It seems that it just occurred! The January 8, 1920 *Index* said the following: "FACTORY WORK BEING PUSHED....Preliminary work of the Great Western Sugar Company for the factory at Mitchell goes forward at what appears to be a satisfactory rate, weather conditions being considered."[49]

The anticipated economic boom brought about by the construction of a factory, and the inherent strain on housing in what at the time were very small towns, was obvious to all concerned. "We are told by people in position to know that Mitchell must have this year three hundred more houses for the use of factory people alone. This means practically doubling the population of Mitchell by people connected with this one industry and correspondingly there will be growth in every direction and expansion in every line of business."[50]

As factory construction picked up the only constraint was the winter weather. Temporary railroad sidings to bring in necessary construction equipment and materials were built. The building of another employee dormitory was undertaken, as was the beginning of the arrival of processing equipment acquired from a failed and quickly closed mill in Missoula, Montana.

Material is coming very rapidly now, both of factory parts from Missoula, Montana, and building materials from other points. Nineteen carloads arrived Tuesday and a greater number of cars on the following day.[51]

There are now in transit on the roads upwards of a hundred carloads of sugar factory stuff, all headed for Mitchell, and materials will be coming in pretty fast from now on.[52]

The *Index*, which kept very close coverage of this important local story, followed up again in the March 11 issue:

There are railroad tracks laid over the grounds making almost every part of the big tract accessible and all along these tracks great quantities of machinery have been unloaded, by two large cranes at work night and day in unloading. So far there has been received—or are in transit—329 cars of stuff, classified as follows: 70 cars of cement, 48 cars brick, 35 cars lumber, 11 cars of newer pipe, 19 cars miscellaneous material and 139 cars of factory parts from Missoula.[53]

Factory construction proceeded at a furious pace with the intention of processing the first beet crop at the Mitchell factory in the fall of 1920. The bad winter weather was a continuing problem. "The bunch [steel workers] is getting ready to raise the main building steel. That is right where the work is today and all effort is being made to start up with this steel on May 1st. Should this be done the boys will be just one month ahead of this part of the work to what was done when the Bayard factory was built."[54]

Alas, this was not to be. The weather in the winter of 1919–20 was apparently not conducive to rapid construction, and the hoped-for record for steel erection failed to materialize. "The boys wanted to start up with the main building steel on May 1st but it was soon evident that this was impossible and at the present writing they are ready to go up with this steel if the weather will permit. It is essential important that when this starts that everything will be ready to go through with the job without having to stop for anything."[55]

In the same article, the status of the Mitchell Great Western employee dormitory is addressed: "The dormitory which will accommodate one hundred men is coming along well, the plasterers being at work and the carpenters getting material in shape to do the finishing. The main office has been bricked in up to the second floor and as soon as the joists and rough flooring is in place the brick work will be completed."[56]

In the August 12 edition, the *Index* notes that the factory is near completion and that the target date for the fall 1920 campaign will be met as planned. The completed factory began receiving its first crop of beets on October 14, 1920. In the first month of the campaign, a man fell inside the factory and was killed. He suffered a skull fracture when doing a job that was not considered dangerous. It is ironic that during the rapid construction phase of the factory, with many activities considered dangerous, no one was killed or apparently seriously injured. The factory set a new record for the total time of construction of eleven months from survey in November 1919 to

Mitchell factory construction crane, April 15, 1920. *Colorado State University, Agricultural and Natural Resources Archive, Archives and Special Collections.*

Mitchell factory construction in snow, April 20, 1920. *Colorado State University, Agricultural and Natural Resources Archive, Archives and Special Collections.*

Above: Mitchell factory construction nearing completion, August 26, 1920. *Colorado State University, Agricultural and Natural Resources Archive, Archives and Special Collections.*

Left: Mitchell dorm under construction, November 12, 1920. *Legacy of the Plains Museum Collection, Gering, Nebraska.*

the first beet slicing in October 1920. When you take into consideration the size of this project and the time it took to complete it, that is amazing! Compare that to the time it would take in twenty-first-century America to get all the required permits and studies completed before anyone could even begin actual construction.

A site plan for the Mitchell factory as it appeared when opened in the fall of 1920 is shown at the top of page 73.

Mitchell dormitory, June 5, 2010. *Photo by Elizabeth Chase.*

Mitchell delivery hi line under construction, summer 1920. *Ziegler Collection Legacy of the Plains Museum.*

Completed Mitchell factory, October 23, 1920. *Ziegler Collection Legacy of the Plains Museum.*

The railroad hi lines were up and operating for the beginning campaign and were an important part of the operation at Mitchell (and the other factories) for many years.

The Mitchell factory was an immediate success. Over 110,000 tons of beets were sliced in the 1920–21 campaign, with an average daily slicing of 1,184 tons. That total was the "third highest among the sixteen operating Great Western Sugar Company factories. In total the Mitchell facility produced nearly 10.5 million 100 pound bags of sugar in it thirty-three campaigns."[57]

The factory and its employees won the efficiency pennant in only its second campaign (1921–22), a goal not achieved again until the 1956–57 campaign. This effort at efficiency did not go unrewarded. "An extra weeks' vacation with pay will be given Mitchell employees this summer in appreciation of the factory's run in the 1921–22 campaign. Edwin Morrison, general superintendent, praised Mitchell's achievement as 'remarkable for reaching the top of the big league of Great Western Factories within two years time.'"[58]

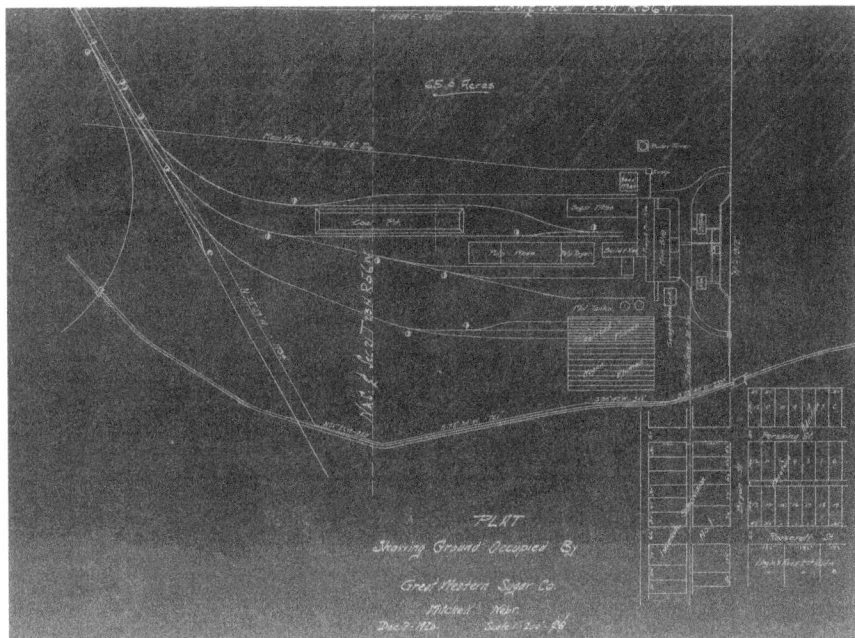

Mitchell factory site plan, December 7, 1920. *Courtesy Western Sugar Co-op.*

Beet wagons and the new hi line. *Ziegler Collection Legacy of the Plains Museum.*

Mitchell Factory hi line showing beets being dumped, circa 1920. Ziegler *Collection Legacy of the Plains Museum.*

Mitchell continued to be a good performer for many years.

Like the Gering factory mentioned earlier, Mitchell was utilized by the War Food Administration in 1944 to dehydrate part of a huge potato crop. With a great deal of friendly competition, Gering slightly outproduced the potato dehydrating efforts of the Mitchell factory, although the Mitchell crew was adamant that they really won! Regardless, the efforts of the two factories in processing these abundant potatoes contributed to the successful war effort.

The factory operated almost continuously for nearly seventy-six years, finally closing for processing after the 1996 sugar campaign. In 2020, the silos at the factory are still being used for bulk sugar storage, but the factory is idle.

MINATARE, NEBRASKA

The story of a sugar beet factory in Minatare is a strange and unusual one. Minatare had apparently been waiting for Great Western to build there after receiving promises of that intention for a few years. Many farmers and businessmen in the Minatare area had grown impatient with Great Western's delay in building there. When the company announced the construction of a plant in Mitchell, some decided to take action themselves. A group of farmers, operating under the banner of the Farmers Union, decided that they were unhappy with what Great Western was paying for their beets and that it had waited too long to build a factory in Minatare. According to a story in the *Minatare Free Press* on January 16, 1920:

> *The Sugar Factory Is Endorsed....The Farmers Union, Wednesday, approved the proposition to construct a Sugar Beet Factory here at Minatare, at a cost of $2,000,000. The stock of the Sugar Beet Factory will be held by members of the Farmers Union.*[59]

> *By constructing a co-operative factory the farmers can manufacture their own sugar from the beets they grow and eliminate the profit which goes to the sugar companies. Thus they can furnish the public with cheaper sugar and receive more of the profit for themselves at the same time.*[60]

At that time, when Great Western had apparently worn out the patience of the Minatare factory promoters and had created conflicts on prices the growers were paid for their beets, some decided to go on their own and build a co-op factory.

> *Maupin tells how Minatare put the factory over....Ever hear about the man who took the milk pail to the pasture and sat down and waited for the cow to back up to be milked? Minatare has, and Minatare is not going to follow his foolish example. Minatare wants a sugar factory and wants it hard enough to go gunning for it. The result of the gunning expedition is that Minatare is more than likely to bag the game. When Great Western Sugar Co. decided to build at Mitchell, Minatare realized that all hope of getting a factory there from that corporation was lost for years to come.*[61]

The huge amounts of money needed to construct a co-op factory were promised to Minatare by Farmers Union chapters across Nebraska at a meeting in Omaha in March. In mid-March, an engineer from Denver approved as viable the site that the co-op was considering. Then everything began to get confusing. In May, Great Western secured its proposed site in Minatare. The local newspaper reacted in a front-page story.

Dumping beets at the Minatare dump before the Minatare factory was built, circa 1920. *Vintage postcard. Author's collection.*

> *Minatare to get two sugar factories....It is an indication of the intention of the Great Western Sugar Co. to beat the Farmers Union Co-Operative Sugar Company to it and build a factory before the farmers can get theirs well under way or that it is an attempt of the Great Western to bluff the farmers out of building their factory.*
> *Many are inclined to believe that the former is the real significance.*[62]

The article goes on to observe that if the purpose of Great Western is only to stop the co-op with no real intention of building after all, it will fail, as selling of the stock for the co-op factory is continuing.

> *Whether or not this means two factories for the town of Minatare remains to be seen, but from present indications such would appear to be the case. The Farmers Co-operative company are selling stock right along for their factory, and are outspoken in favor of building their factory regardless of the action of the Great Western, and the people down there are elated over the prospect of having two sugar factories instead of one.*[63]

The article continued with the following observation and a very optimistic prediction:

The decision of the company to erect their next factory at Minatare seems to have been taken after considering the prospects at Torrington [WY].[64]

One thing is now certain and that is that the sugar industry in this valley is in its infancy and that every town in the valley will have a factory sooner or later is an assured fact. We predict that inside of ten years there will be ten more sugar factories in the North Platte Valley.[65]

With that extremely and ultimately incorrect, optimistic forecast, the article concluded.

Three weeks later, Great Western finally announced that the next mill that it would build was a sugar factory at Minatare, Nebraska. With the first announcements made in late July 1920, the factory was to be similar in design and slicing capacity to the mills in Gering, Bayard and Mitchell. This size had by this time been determined by the sugar industry to be the most economical in management of both production and labor than larger factories. A site just southwest of the town, south of the Burlington Railroad tracks, was determined to be ideal. It was fairly level and would require minimal dirt work. It was adjacent to the railroad and also close to the North Platte River for the water needed for sugar production. Construction was to begin on another employee dormitory and other houses to be ready in time for factory operation in the fall of 1921.

Although there was obviously competition between the towns in the valley for the sugar factory, it became easy to feel good about another factory being built in another town, especially when your town's factory was nearing completion. "Great Western at Minatare....The people of Mitchell rejoice with Minatare in the prospect for greater development which has come to them."[66]

It was obviously much easier to be congratulatory to Minatare on getting a factory when yours (in Mitchell) was nearly complete! Construction work began almost immediately. For the next few months, progress was made on some of the buildings at the factory site as well as on the dormitory. In late December, all that optimism changed. Outside forces were at play in the sugar market in late 1920, and the price of sugar collapsed. The demand for sugar went down with it. Construction on the Minatare factory and another at Johnstown, Colorado, was suspended indefinitely on December 14. "The announcement disclosed that even at lower sugar prices the demand is slack, the company having sold only a little over 400,000 [one-hundred-pound] bags whereas normal sales at this date were estimated at thrice that figure."[67]

Initial Minatare factory construction, October 28, 1920. *Colorado State University, Agricultural and Natural Resources Archive, Archives and Special Collections.*

Since the company had already paid the highest price for the preceding year's crop, the lack of sales of that crop after processing had created a cash flow problem for the company. "Will Resume Later....The district manager (Edmund Simmons) made it clear that while he could give no promise for the future in an official capacity, it was his private opinion that work on the Minatare plant would be resumed in time to be ready for the 1922 beet season."[68]

Work on some of the nearly finished structures would be completed. The community, as observed in the next week's newspaper, was still optimistic that this would be only a one-year delay. As stated in an editorial: "Steady Minatare! The plant was, according to original plans, to have begun operation in 1921. Now, according to the changed plans, it will be ready in 1922—a year later—instead. There is no certainty as to this."[69]

As usual, the projection for resumption of construction in 1921 proved to be flawed. It would not happen until five years later, in 1926. One of the buildings completed before the suspension of constriction was the bagged sugar warehouse. An article in the local newspaper mentions how much sugar the company had stored there. "Manager Vandemoer of Great Westerns Minatare interests says that he has on hand at the local warehouse approximately 212,000 sacks of sugar, each sack weighing 100 pounds."[70]

Despite the lack of progress on completing the mill at that time, Great Western was putting some of the structures that had been completed to use.

An interesting subject when considering the time of the suspension is what happened to the Farmers Union Co-operative Sugar Company. One would assume that the collapsing sugar market had affected its plans—and its stock sales. If not, why would it not have rushed to build its mill, or maybe purchase the incomplete Great Western facility? The co-op dissolved the organization in 1921 and returned the invested money to the farmers involved. This was not the ultimate end of the idea for a Farmers Co-op plant at Minatare, or somewhere else in the valley, as the growers' dissatisfaction with the contract prices being offered by Great Western continued in 1928. After a number of meetings with growers and local businessmen, nothing seemed to transpire. Again, as in the earlier project, the idea ultimately did not move forward.

After a wait of a few years, serious talk of completing the factory began to surface in late summer 1925. An article in the *Sugar Press* in October 1925 included the following statement from W.D. Lippitt, first vice-president and general manager at Minatare:

> *Construction of the Great Western Sugar Companies factory at Minatare Nebraska will be resumed at once and work will be carried forward to complete the plant in time to handle the beet crop of 1926.*[71]

> *The very serious condition surrounding the sugar industry, which forced a stoppage of construction in 1920, will be recalled. We had entered upon the erection of the Minatare plant early that year when no one could have foretold the extraordinary slump in sugar prices which led to cessation of construction activity.*[72]

In an article in the *Minatare Free Press* on October 8, Lippitt elaborated further on the conditions that caused the previous halt of construction in 1920. "That which we had begun in July 1920 with only the thought of pushing to prompt completion became an impossibility inside of a few months. The bottom dropped out of the sugar business. Our company lost between nine and ten million dollars inside of one year."[73]

With the revelation of the catastrophic losses suffered by Great Western in 1920 (equivalent to a loss of between $114 million and $127 million in 2018 terms), one could speculate that the company was on very shaky ground and near total collapse. Cessation of construction in 1920 was probably the only course open to it. "Construction of the Minatare factory was begun in 1920 and before the disastrous slump in the sugar market forced the temporary abandonment of construction; the company had completed the warehouse, lime house, offices, dormitory and nearly a score of residences in the city to house their employees."[74]

The Minatare factory was to be a wet pulp factory, which was more desirable to some farmers as a source of feed for livestock. Though similar in many ways to the last three factories completed in the valley, Minatare will "embody all the new and improved methods discovered since the erection of those mills."[75] The new plant's machinery was to be state of the art; the delay might actually be beneficial to its success.

Beneficial side effects of the resumption of construction appeared almost immediately when an announcement was made that the old Roland Hotel would be renovated and renamed the Austin Hotel. The economic benefits were apparent as "a number of other buildings on Main Street are being planned for immediate construction, owing to the crowded conditions that exist at present. There is not a vacant building in town and any new business entering the field here will necessarily have to erect buildings."[76]

Construction resumed the last week in October. As Great Western moved toward final completion of its long-dormant project, another player, Holly Sugar Corporation, was rumored to be interested in building a factory in Minatare as well. Up to this time, both Holly and Great Western had for the most part staked out their territories and did not intrude on the area of the other. If this plan were to be carried to completion, it would begin a war between the two companies which up to this point both had sought to avoid. Holly had paid growers more for the 1924 crop than Great Western did, and many growers were not happy about that. It appears that some may have solicited Holly to enter into GW territory so that they might get a better deal on their beets with some competition in the market. In the local daily newspaper, the competition exploded onto the front page.

> FIGHT STILL ON BETWEEN GREAT WESTERN AND HOLLY COMPANIES FOR CONTROL OF BEET ACREAGE....*The fight between the Great Western and Holly sugar companies for control of this valley, and what one or both of them are liable to do next seems to be the main points of interest over the valley these days.*

> *The Holly people are keeping their activities pretty much under cover.*
> *It was rumored yesterday that they had purchased an 80 acre tract at*
> *Minatare for a mill site.*
>
> *In commenting on the situation on October 18, the* Scottsbluff Star-
> Herald *stated that the Cooperative Beet Growers association had offered*
> *to furnish the Holly people some 7,000 or 8,000 acres and that the sugar*
> *company agreed that "the price to be paid for these beets shall be equal to the*
> *best price paid for beets in 1925 by any company in Colorado, Wyoming,*
> *Montana and Nebraska.*[77]

This apparently unexpected offer created potential problems for Great Western. The plot thickened the next day, when another front-page article in the same paper stated the following:

> *The first definite public indication came yesterday from Holly Sugar*
> *Corporation that the many rumors regarding their erection of a factory*
> *at Minatare were true when they completed the purchase of the Charlie*
> *Morrill place just west of that city the sale of which has been rumored*
> *several times and as often dismissed.*
>
> *Yesterday about noon however the transaction was completed, this fact*
> *being confirmed by Mr. Morrill and officials of the company.*[78]

While all of this was transpiring, Great Western was moving along with completing its Minatare factory. All through the months of November and December 1925, the local weeklies and the *Daily Star-Herald* had numerous stories about Great Westerns construction and whether or not Holly was sincere it its plans to also build at Minatare. An article in the *Minatare Free Press* on November 12 reported that the "SUGAR WAR CARRIED INTO HOLLY TERRITORY."[79] The article went on to report that officials from Great Western had been touring the western slope of the Rockies in Colorado, which heretofore had been exclusively Holly Sugar territory, to explore the possibility of a Great Western factory somewhere in that area. It speculated that this consideration was in retaliation for Holly looking to invade Great Western territory with a mill at Minatare.

The saga of the Holly plant continued with another *Star-Herald* article on November 15, when it was reported that it was rumored that Holly had purchased the Fairfield farm near Minatare for a plant. This contradicted the earlier reports from two weeks prior that said the Morrill property had been purchased! On November 20, the *Gering Courier* stated the following:

DENVER PAPER SAYS HOLLY CO. TO BUILD.... The definite statement of the new factory construction of the Holly Sugar company in the North Platte Valley is definitely set forth in the article which appeared Tuesday in the Denver Post: Construction of two beet sugar factories by the Wyoming-Nebraska Sugar company, all of whose stock is owned by the Holly Sugar Corporation, will begin at once as the result of a deal for a loan of $2,500,000 made by A.E. Carlton bankers.

One of these two plants will be in Minatare where the Great Western sugar company is building a large factory and the other at Torrington, Wyo.[80]

As Holly dithered in its final decision, Great Western continued its construction. The *Minatare Free Press* reported on November 25 that the dormitory was almost ready to be lived in and the office complete in about two more weeks. The next day, the paper reported that it was almost ready to pour concrete for the main factory floor and that there were now over seventy men working at the site. On the twenty-ninth, the *Star-Herald* updated the status again: "READY TO START THE MAIN BUILDING MINATARE FACTORY.....As soon as the water intake is completed, the plans will arrive and construction started on the huge slab on which the main factory rests. This slab will be constructed of reinforced concrete, will be 65 feet wide and 270 feet long and vary in thickness from one to three feet."[81]

The plant construction was moving along quickly now; a few days later, it was announced that the dormitory was open for business and the final blueprints for the main factory building had arrived. The waters continued to be muddied in town when, on December 18, it was again reported in the *Gering Courier* that Holly had purchased the Fairfield farm west of town for its factory—as had been rumored about three weeks earlier—as well as part of the originally reported Morrill property. The front page of the November 17 *Minatare Free Press* featured a huge headline stating "HOLLY TO BUILD AT MINATARE."[82] The article went on to state the following:

FACTORY CONSTRUCTION TO START AT ONCE....MODERN MILL TO BE ERECTED ON THE C.A. MORRILL FARM SOUTHWEST OF TOWN....While part of the machinery for the Minatare factory will be sent from the Holly Corporations plant at Huntington Beach, Calif. the company has ordered that any part of that equipment that is not strictly up to modern requirement, be replaced.[83]

The article went on to detail that Burlington Railroad was in the process of extending siding on to the factory site to expedite the unloading of material and equipment as it arrived. The railroad had already approved the track layout for the proposed factory. Construction on the new plant was to officially begin on January 1. As reported in the *Gering Courier*: "Local beet growers anticipate one of the worst sugar wars in the history of the sugar beet company next year, the Holly and the Great Western companies having given indication they will launch competitive fights."[84]

As 1925 was drawing to a close, the weather seemed to be a common enemy of both companies, delaying the beginning of one and the completion of another of the mill projects. On Christmas Eve, it was reported that the Burlington had begun work on grading for the siding leading to the Holly property. Holly also announced that it would have its own beet spurs and beet dumps and that construction on those would begin in the spring when the weather permitted.

In the early days of January 1926, the fight for control of the sugar beet crop in the Minatare area continued, but not for long! The January 9 issue of the *Scottsbluff Star-Herald* reported:

WORK PROGRESSING ON FACTORY SITES AT TWO-MILL TOWN....Great Western going ahead despite the fact that the weather had been unfavorable....In spite of the fact that this part of the country is experiencing the worst winter in years, work is going right ahead on the construction work on the Great Western factory and on the spur tracks leading to the Holly site records the Minatare Free Press.[85]

Present plans call for four tracks leading to the Holly site in addition to a passing track which will be better than one-half mile in length and parallel the main line just north of the Holly site. As soon as these tracks are completed, materials for the construction of the Holly plant will begin to arrive and work started at once so the mill will be completed in time for the 1926 crop.[86]

Burlington track layers are also at work on the Great Western site constructing two temporary construction tracks and four permanent tracks.[87]

This breakneck pace of construction for one mill was about to come to an abrupt halt. In a huge front-page headline in the January 17 *Scottsbluff Star-Herald*, the end of the Holly project was announced.

HOLLY WILL NOT BUILD SUGAR FACTORY AT MINATARE….Duplication of plants would be "Economic Waste" to be paid eventually by growers…. Will complete Torrington plant with increased capacity but will return contracts for 20,000 acres to growers of Minatare section….With the suddenness of a bomb out of a clear blue sky now comes the announcement of the Holly Sugar Company that they have withdrawn their plans for building a factory at Minatare."[88]

We presume that this withdrawal means the cessation of hostilities and the silencing of the big guns of war, for this valley has likely seen one of the most spectacular "sugar wars" that has been had in the country in some time.[89]

In the same issue of the paper on page six, Holly Sugar placed a large ad headlined "Announcement by Holly Sugar Corp."[90] In the ad, the company cites that in the last four years beet production in southeast Wyoming had increased from 13,000 to 125,000 tons. Those beets were being shipped to a plant of theirs in Sheridan, Wyoming. Transportation costs to that mill were destroying any profit from the crop. The company goes on to blame Great Western for interfering with its plans for contracting beets in the valley. The decision to finally complete the Minatare plant after a five-year delay by Great Western was a concern for Holly, which feared it would result in an insufficient supply of beets for its Torrington plant, which it was building at this same time. The ad goes on to state, "Realizing that two factories at one location represent an economic waste, which eventually someone, and quite likely the beet growers, will ultimately pay, we have decided to abandon our plan for factory construction [at Minatare], and return to the growers their contracts."[91]

In a scathing front-page editorial by A.J. Shumway in the Wednesday edition the same week, the *Star-Herald* editor elaborates on what they think may have transpired relating to Holly's decision to not proceed. They smell a rat in the whole process and say so in many more words.

BLOWING UP OF HOLLY IN VALLEY TO BE EXPECTED. The expected (or the unexpected) has happened and Sunday morning's Star-Herald *told the story so far as the interested sugar companies care to have published. For "economic reasons"—so says the Holly Corporation in its advertisement. In other words, it means that the amalgamation of the big interests who have used the farmers, the cooperative beet growers association and the businessmen of the valley as a means to an end. It was ever thus. "The people be damned."*[92]

Just what the deal is between the two companies will probably never be known, but, reading between the lines one would naturally think that the Holly Corporation has agreed to keep out of Nebraska providing the Great Western will let Wyoming and western Colorado alone. Just what effect this deal will have on the building of a factory between Gering and the Wyoming line by the Great Western will develop later. It is not probable that it will build as far west as Lyman, which it was thought the intention, especially if there is an agreement to keep out of Wyoming. The factory will probably be constructed more in the center of the beet territory. It is possible of course that there will be no factory built.[93]

The article goes on to conclude, "But one thing is sure and history has simply repeated itself and proven conclusively that the general public has no rights which big business is bound to respect."[94]

Although the animosity displayed in the editorial proved to be overly pessimistic regarding the construction of the Lyman plant, the impression of a deal was reinforced in the next day's *Star-Herald* by an article headlined "HOLLY WITHDRAWAL BOOST STOCK SALE OF GREAT WESTERN."[95]

The article elaborates on the result of the Holly withdrawal from Minatare, having the effect of increasing Great Western's stock price about 1½ percent. Holly stock was steady on the market, which the article attributed to the fact that its withdrawal from the Minatare project would help them avoid a large capital expenditure.

After the false alarm for Great Western of a Holly factory at Minatare and the subsequent abandonment of that project, Great Western proceeded in earnest with the completion of its plant there.

In the October 8, 1926 issue of the *Star-Herald*, the newspaper reports that the Minatare factory will finally begin beet slicing that day. The first campaign was expected to last until January. An article in the November 1926 issue of Great Western's *Sugar Press* states:

North Platter Valley Welcomes Minatare—Dedication of massive refinery in presence of 2,500 people represents fulfillment of years of hope and effort.[96]

Mr. Lippitt [general manager] *delivered a frank statement of the Company's policies, congratulated the community of achieving its aims and expressed confidence that disagreement between beet grower and manufacturer was being rapidly displaced by co-operation and fuller understanding of each other's problems.*[97]

Minatare factory construction when resumed, March 20, 1926. *Colorado State University, Agricultural and Natural Resources Archive, Archives and Special Collections.*

The Minatare plant was now complete and in full operation.

The future, however, would not be kind to the sugar factory at Minatare. After only fifteen years of operation, it was announced that the plant would not operate for the 1941 sugar campaign. An article in the *Minatare Free Press* of May 8, 1941, read, "MINATARE FACTORY WILL NOT OPERATE COMING CAMPAIGN."[98] In the article, the sugar company announced that, due to market conditions and allotments of the maximum amount of acres that could be grown for that season according to the Department of Agriculture, it could not operate the plant. In some nine of fifteen previous seasons, over 250,000 acres of beets had been raised and in three years the acreage had exceeded 300,000 acres. This decision was part of the federal government's attempt to place a floor under the price of sugar. The article continued with a summation of Minatare's troubled history.

> *The factory at Minatare has had a hectic life from the very start. It will be remembered by many of the old timers that the Great Western Sugar*

Minatare factory construction after resumption, August 17, 1926. *Colorado State University, Agricultural and Natural Resources Archive, Archives and Special Collections.*

Minatare factory shortly after completion, fall 1926. *Legacy of the Plains Museum Collection, Gering, Nebraska.*

Burlington locomotive spots cars on the Minatare hi line, circa 1930. *Legacy of the Plains Museum Collection, Gering, Nebraska.*

Above: Hopper cars of beets unloading from the hi-line at Minatare factory, circa 1930. *Legacy of the Plains Museum Collection, Gering, Nebraska.*

Opposite: Minatare factory site map. *Minatare City Street map 1929. Courtesy of West Nebraska Family Research & History Center Collection.*

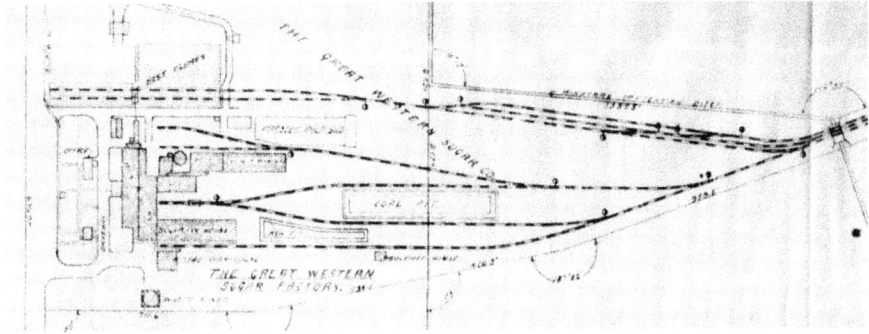

Company planned to erect their first factory at this point to be in the very heart of the beet raising section, with more acres suitable for beets directly tributary to this point than at any other point in the valley—a situation that still exists. However, decision was made to locate the first mill at Scottsbluff and Minatare lost out for the first time.

About twenty years ago the Farmers Sugar Company was organized here and before the Farmers could get things underway to start their factory the Great Western announced they were ready to enter the field and started construction here. A warehouse and a few small buildings were constructed and after a few months of work…conditions of the sugar market and other conditions would not permit them to finish the mill they had started to build here. Thus Minatare lost her second factory.

Then along about 1925 Bill Austin came along with a plan of interesting the Holly company to build a factory here.…Holly went so far as to build a railroad spur to their proposed site and started excavating for the mill when Great Western raised the price of sugar beets $2.00 per ton throughout their territory. In a few days the Holly announced their withdrawal from the field and thus Minatare lost her third sugar factory.

Almost at the same time the Holly announced they would build a factory here the Great Western also announced that they would complete the factory started by them a few years previous. By the time the next beet harvest rolled around Minatare was able to realize a dream of many years—an actual sugar factory in operation in the community.

Since 1926 each year the whistle has sounded and men started the work of making sugar from beets grown in the factory district.…But on this day, May 8, 1941.…Minatare lost her fourth factory.[99]

The next day's edition of the *Scottsbluff Star-Herald* featured an editorial that placed the blame for the closure in the lap of the federal government and big-money interests in New York. "What makes the blow all more stinging is the injustice being done to a domestic agricultural industry when its operations are arbitrarily restricted by a government bureau for the benefit of a similar industry operated in offshore islands but largely financed by, and working to the profit of New York capitol."[100]

They continued to state that a government bureau, the Department of Agriculture, had unofficially decided to try to kill the domestic sugar industry to protect the sugar cane industries in Cuba, Puerto Rico and other tropical growing regions. The Minatare paper reported on May 29 that it was the last day for the Minatare factory. It stated that the closure will leave a scar on the community. "It means for the sugar folks, after fifteen years of association here to move to new communities, make new friends, and endeavor to adapt themselves to their new surroundings. In future years, if the Minatare mill is to operate, a few of the families may possibly move back here, but the chances are that the new operation force will for the most part be strangers."[101]

The optimistic observation of a future reopening of the Minatare mill was never to be realized. The mill was closed for good. In the spring of 1953, the demolition of the main factory building commenced. In researching at the Minatare library regarding the sugar factory there, I found a group of twenty-five black-and-white snapshots of the demolition of the main factory building. The photographer is unknown, as is who had donated them to the library. They were probably taken by someone in the crew, as one of the photos has the following written on the back of it: "Sherman A Swift crane operator from Lovell, WY in 1953 taking down the sugar factory at Minatare, NE."[102] The crew was supervised by Henry Kupilik, assistant master mechanic, and crane operator S.A. Swift, who, along with their workers, demolished the main factory building in a short period of time.

It appears that much of the structural steel was salvaged. There are at least two photos in the collection of steel girders being loaded into railroad gondolas and another of steel being stacked on the ground.

I cannot determine exactly how much of the complex was demolished at that time other than the main factory building. As of 2020, the main office building, the main warehouse, the water tower and at least part of the pressed pulp silo are still standing and in use by the Silver Spur Cattle Company as part of its feedlot. A short distance away, north of the Burlington Northern Santa Fe Railroad tracks, the old Great Western dormitory still is in use as an apartment building.

Minatare main factory building demolition, 1953. *Minatare Library Collection.*

Only the steel frame remains after the removal of the brick Minatare main factory building, 1953. *Minatare Library Collection.*

Another view of the demolition of the main factory building at Minatare. *Minatare Library Collection.*

Loading steel girders into a railroad gondola for reuse elsewhere, 1953. *Minatare Library Collection.*

Silver Spur Cattle Company office, old Minatare factory office, 2019. *Photo by the author.*

Old Minatare Great Western dormitory, 2019. *Photo by the author.*

The story of the sugar industry in Minatare is one of hope and optimism, which turned into frustration and some patient waiting. Those hopes were dashed and resurrected several time as a few different projects started and stopped; finally, one resumed and was carried forward to completion. That long-awaited success was short-lived; the factory the community of Minatare had pursued for so long and finally achieved only lasted a short fifteen years. Minatare has never recovered from that loss.

LYMAN, NEBRASKA

The story of the Great Western Sugar Company factory in Lyman, Nebraska, is another one of several years of rumors that eventually grew to fruition. In a front-page article, the *Star-Herald* said:

> *NEW TOWN OF CALDWELL, NEBRAKSA ON THE MAP; FACTORY TALK....*
> *Following the announcement last week that the Union Pacific planned to make an extension from the end of line just west of Haig, to Goshen Hole country* [Wyoming], *matters have developed rather thick and fast.*
> *There are persistent rumors having as their principal motive the planned erection of a sugar factory at some point along a line of the*

extension, but up to present at least these rumors have been rather nebulous and hazy to track down to any determined source. There is little doubt but at some point a sugar factory will eventually be erected somewhere in that region to take care of the increased acreage of beets that will feature the southern development, but whether the sugar interests will show the same agility as the men of finance have displayed is a matter so far of speculation.[103]

Caldwell was an early competitor of what would become the village of Lyman. The proposed site is about three miles southeast of present-day Lyman. It had a bank chartered but apparently never built and plans for construction of a town, but most of the idea dried up when the Union Pacific built west from Haig and passed to the north of the proposed site of Caldwell, thus dooming the planned community.

The rumors of a new factory in the western part of Scotts Bluff County persisted for a few years. Those rumors began to finally be confirmed in the fall of 1925 when a front-page article in the *Gering Courier* proclaimed: "ANOTHER FACTORY FOR THE VALLEY."[104] The article continued: "Great Western to build factory west of Gering to handle crop in 1927....Spurs will be built from Gering and Lyman to open up territory coming under irrigation for the first time....The location of the proposed factory is stated to be 'on the Union Pacific railroad at some point to be determined by the company, west of Gering and in Nebraska.'"[105]

A significant portion of the front page, and much of that issue of the *Courier*, is devoted to information regarding another factory on the south side of the river in an as yet unnamed location. There are several requirements that the growers in the Gering valley west to the Wyoming line had to meet before another factory would be built. The same article continues:

The acreage required to ensure erection of a new factory and railway spurs on the south side of the North Platte River is being sought in the territory from Brockhoff dump (a few miles east of Gering on the existing Union Pacific line) to the Nebraska-Wyoming state line including both old and new irrigation districts therein.[106]

That territory already grows a normal crop of more than 9,000 acres, including the existing dumps of Brockhoff, Gering, Siding 1, Smith, Baileyville, Joyce and Lyman. The additional acreage is easily expected to be drawn from the newly-irrigated lands under the Ft. Laramie unit of the North Platte Project, including the Cedar Valley south of Gering, the Mitchell Valley and the Lyman District within Scotts Bluff county, particularly in view of the proposed "beet spurs."[107]

The article continues:

The factory would be commenced in 1926 and unless some new unforeseen and serious conditions should arise, in the meanwhile, would be completed in time to handle the crop grown during 1927. Aiding in the development would be the proposed Gering spur of 8.6 miles in length to be finished in 1926 and the first half of the Lyman spur to be completed in the same year. An extension of the Lyman spur would be added in 1927.[108]

This article concludes with the information of the required acreage for the project to continue: "The provision that not less than 12,000 acres in 1926 and 15,000 acres in 1927 and the three subsequent years be contracted to assure the new construction was explained as a minimum basis."[109]

Those persons representing the growers in the included area who were in attendance at the announcement seemed very confident that meeting the required acreage with contracts from the growers would not be a problem. The information contained in the proposal is formalized in a letter from Great Western assistant general manager Edmund Simmons that is printed elsewhere in the same issue. Another front-page article reports that on the first day after the announcement, a total of 3,500 acres had already been signed up for the 1927 crop year from the newly opened irrigated territory in the Fort Laramie–Gering district.

The importance of the sugar industry to the North Platte Valley is detailed in another article on page three of the same issue, which says in part:

Too well known to bear extended discussion are the benefits that follow the erection of a beet sugar factory, the development of a market for new crops, the production of livestock by-product feeds, the increase in population, in revenues for government and school purposes, and the many other improvements which seem in a peculiar manner attached to such factory and the railroad construction in this valley....One has only to look back at conditions in the valley before the advent of the sugar industry to appreciate the place it has made for itself in the communities.[110]

On page two of the same issue were duplicate editorials from four local newspapers. Comments from H.J. Wisner of the *Scottsbluff Star-Herald*, T.C. Palmer of the *Gering Midwest*, A.B. Wood of the *Gering Courier* and a comment from an unidentified writer from the *Scottsbluff Republican* all spoke in glowing terms of what the proposed development would mean to the county, especially on the south side of the North Platte River. Those feelings can be best summarized by a comment by Palmer: "The building of an empire in the valley is but started. It will take years to complete it."[111]

The irrigation canals built in the late nineteenth and early twentieth centuries brought precious water to the semiarid hi plains of Wyo-Braska and provided the conditions for growing sugar beets. There is little doubt that without the development of the beet sugar industry in the North Platte Valley between 1909 and 1927, the North Platte Valley would be much less than it is today. I'm not sure an empire ever developed here!

Additional confirmation of a factory west of Gering came in an announcement first reported in the *Sugar Press* on page eleven of the February issue. On May 28, 1926, the Gering Courier reported: "FACTORY SURVEY IS GOING ON AT LYMAN....Time approaches for announcement of the new site....All indications thus far seem to point to Lyman as the site for the new sugar factory which the Great Western Sugar Company some time ago announced it would erect at a point on the Union Pacific railroad somewhere west of Gering."[112]

It took about two more months before Great Western finally confirmed that Lyman would indeed be the site it had chosen. A large ad in the *Courier* on July 30, 1926, stated:

New Great Western Factory Announced to be at Lyman....Having completed a careful and exhaustive survey of the entire situation the company has arrived at the definite and final conclusion that the most satisfactory location will be at a point adjacent to the town of Lyman, Nebraska, and takes this opportunity of announcing that construction of a plant at that point will commence in the near future. Signed W.D. Lippitt, Vice President and General Manager

Due to a severe lack of available housing, one of the first things Great Western had to do was provide temporary housing for the crew who would do the construction. In the August 20, 1926 issue of the *Gering Courier*, it is announced that "Bob Miller Annexes His Fourth Sugar Factory in Valley."[113]

Miller and his construction crew had just completed the new Great Western plant at Ovid, Colorado, and they were on the way to Lyman to build that mill. He and his crew had built the Gering, Mitchell and Bayard plants in the valley over the last decade.

As with most of the other valley factories, Great Western commenced to build a dormitory, but this one was not as close to the factory as some of the others. It was built downtown, about half a mile from the factory site. The building is of a much different design than the other dormitories in the valley. The building still exists in 2019 and appears to be utilized for storage.

Although Great Western had built a number of houses for employees at other sites in the valley, something a little different was done at Lyman. There, they actually built a very nice, well-planned neighborhood just a short distance south of the factory and the railroad main line. Although the subdivision was formally named the Park Place Addition, most people apparently referred to it as "Sugar Town." The sugar company elaborated on the beauty of the development in an article in the *Sugar Press*.

Home sites in Lyman Express unique Features....Beauty and utility will go hand in hand in the development of Park Place Addition at Lyman, where

Lyman Beet factory construction of labor housing, 1926. *Legacy of the Plains Museum Collection, Gering, Nebraska.*

Wet hopper at Lyman sugar factory under construction, August 22, 1927. *Legacy of the Plains Museum Collection, Gering, Nebraska.*

Lyman GW dormitory under construction, 1926. *Legacy of the Plains Museum Collection, Gering, Nebraska.*

Lyman GW dormitory, June 2019. *Photo by the author.*

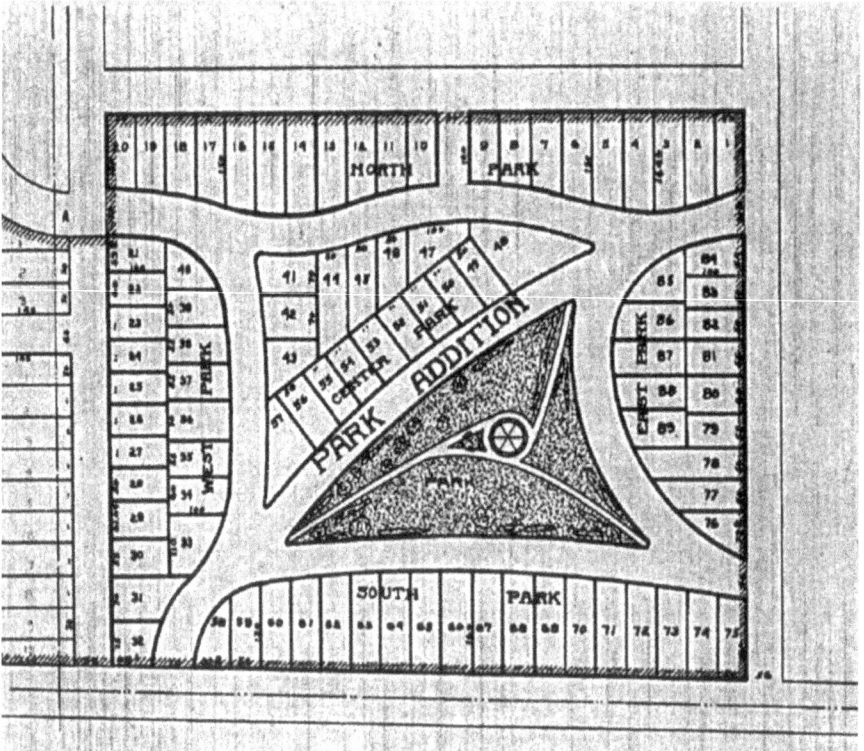

"Park Addition" or "Sugar town" site plan. *Courtesy Western Sugar Co-op.*

E.E.DETERMAN   O. P. DITTMAN

E. F. WOLFE   R.G.MILLER A.URBACH
ASS'T. SUPT.   CONST. SUPT. SUGAR END FOREMAN

N.C.VANDEMOER AVERY CLARK C.C.SCHREP- WM.JENSEN E.E.DETERMAN
MANAGER   SUPT. FERMAN M. MECHANIC TIMEKEEPER

WM. JENSEN   R.J.KANE   H. E.FAUST T. D. STEVENS
MASTER MECHANIC ENGINEER   HEAD PIPE FITTER FIELDMAN

GW pictures of some of the homes it built in the Park Addition. *Courtesy Western Sugar Co-op.*

> *nineteen attractive houses expressing Dutch colonial and English influences are well under way.... Company houses occupy alternate lots most of which face streets enclosing an irregular park. Curving roadways give a pleasing effect to the general composition and there is not the slightest suggestion of the stereotyped. Edmund Simmons is responsible for the design of this 20-acre division which is a far cry from typical factory town layouts.*[114]

Most of the homes in **Park Place** are still occupied in 2020, and most of them are well maintained for houses about ninety years old. The entire neighborhood is still very livable.

The article goes on to report that substantial progress is being made on the factory construction. Weather would play a part in delaying some of the work over the winter, but the plant was still on schedule for completion for the 1927 beet harvest.

No.37, Lyman, Neb. Feb. 7 -27
Sugar Warehouse.

Lyman factory construction, February 7, 1927. *Colorado State University, Agricultural and Natural Resources Archive, Archives and Special Collections.*

Lyman factory construction in the snow, February 15, 1927. *Colorado State University, Agricultural and Natural Resources Archive, Archives and Special Collections.*

Lyman factory construction, May 21, 1927. *Colorado State University, Agricultural and Natural Resources Archive, Archives and Special Collections.*

The Lyman factory was completed in time for the 1927 beet harvest as promised. In an identical article published in several local newspapers at the end of September 1927, it was stated:

> *Newest Gwesco Sugar Mill, at Lyman.....Completion at Lyman of the Great Western Sugar companies new beet sugar factory finds twenty-one company plants, six of which are in Nebraska thundering into action in the biggest sugar-making campaign in the company's history.*[115]

> *Since July 29, 1926 which chronicled Great Western's announcement to build at Lyman, to slicing of the first beets, scheduled for next Friday, construction has progressed with unparalleled efficiency. The plant resembles Great Westerns plants opened last year at Ovid, Colo. and Minatare, Nebr. It is one of the few beets slicing plants in the world driven entirely by electricity from a single giant turbine engine. The Lyman factory differs from the conventional sugar mill in having no high-lines for beet delivery. Beets are unloaded from cars by a belt conveyor which carries them directly into storage sheds built over the flumes.*[116]

One week later, the company sponsored a housewarming at the new plant on October 8. An article in the newspaper the day before cites some of the things visitors to the housewarming will see that are different from most other Great Western mills.

Lyman has no smokestack, which with the water tower, have come to be an inevitable part of the beet sugar factory's skyline....Unloading of beets at the Lyman plant is performed in a unique way. Wagon deliveries are received over a Lynch type unloader direct to piles; then forked onto moveable belt conveyors and deposited in water flumes. Railroad deliveries, usually seen on elevated "highline" tracks are dumped over a single hopper and the beets are covered to a traveling bridge which deposits them over the flumes.[117]

Six large buildings are located on the site, the main house being 54 feet wide, 260 feet long and 75 feet high. The sugar warehouse, with a capacity of 281,000,000 pounds, is 65 feet wide and 302 feet long.[118]

Lyman factory after completion, circa 1930. *Colorado State University, Agricultural and Natural Resources Archive, Archives and Special Collections.*

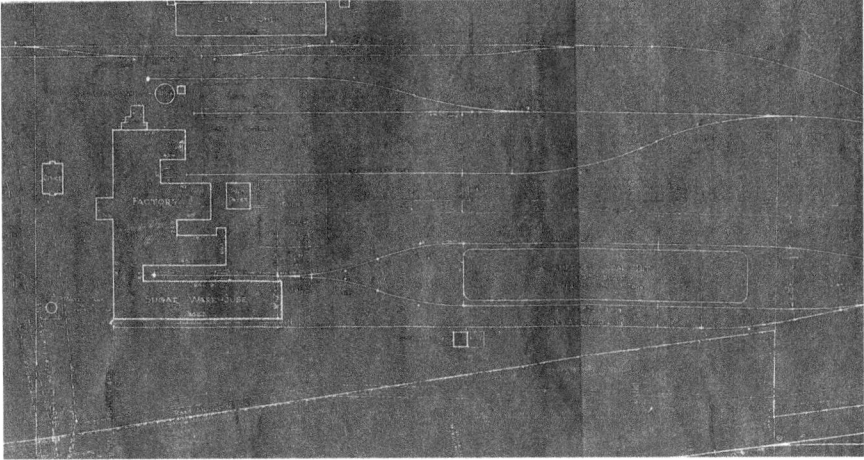

Lyman factory site map, circa 1930. *Union Pacific Line Map. Author's collection.*

Like its recently completed sister mill in Minatare, the future of the factory at Lyman was short. Even though it was one of the most modern and technologically advanced mills in the Great Western family, it, too, was completed shortly before market conditions and government sugar policy began a slow decline in demand for the U.S. manufactured product. As more sugar was imported and the Department of Agriculture reduced the amount of sugar beets it would allow to be planted, the eventual doom of both plants was not too far down the road.

At a time when one would think that demand would be greatest due to World War II, the plant had operations suspended in 1943. This is hard to figure, since there was such a shortage of sugar in the domestic market during the war that it was one of the commodities that the Office of Price Administration (OPA) rationed. Unlike the Minatare mill, which was closed for good in 1941 and never reopened, Lyman did get a reprieve of sorts in 1947 when the mill was reopened. That reprieve was short-lived, however, and the factory was closed for good in 1949. The mill at Lyman, a multimillion-dollar investment, had operated for a short lifetime of about fifteen years.

The final nail in the coffin of the Lyman factory was announced in a news story in June 1949: "Lyman Sugar Plant Is Ordered Closed—Lack of Beet Acreage Is Given as Reason for Not Operating." District manager P.H. McMaster stated, "Contracts signed with the company have resulted in the lowest beet acreage in Nebraska since 1918"[119]

D.J. Roach, executive vice-president of GW, said that "beets grown near there would be handled at receiving stations as usual and processed at the Gering, Mitchell, Scottsbluff and Bayard, Nebr. plants."[120]

Questions abound as to why the factories at Minatare and Lyman were even built. By the mid- to late 1920s, there were probably some early indications that the worldwide sugar market was softening. Were they built because of overly optimistic local promotion, or because it was felt that the sugar factory building boom would go on forever? Few if any could see that the stock market crash in 1929 would indicate the beginning of a worldwide economic depression that would exacerbate the lack of demand for sugar, since people had much less money to spend. The real reasons will probably never be known. All we do know for sure is that there was a lot of investment by communities, growers, railroads and the Great Western Company to have such a short investment lifespan.

By 2019, the main Lyman factory building had been demolished and replaced with a steel building. The sugar warehouse, the office building and the water tower are still standing. The main factory building was used by a company called House of Hose from 1969 to the 1980s. It was a manufacturer of hydraulic hose couplings and many different types of hose assemblies. They relocated to Scottsbluff a number of years ago.

Lyman GW factory office, June 2019. *Photo by the author.*

TORRINGTON, WYOMING

A decade-long pursuit came to fruition on October 26, 1926, when the first sugar beets were unloaded at the brand-new Holly Sugar Factory in Torrington, Wyoming. After many years of frustrating false alarms about a factory being built there, the receiving of the first beets confirmed that the efforts had not been in vain. The factory was a huge success and would operate for almost a century, finally ceasing beet processing at the end of the 2018 campaign. Those efforts began in the late 1910s, and the story of that effort is a long and frustrating one. Let's go back to the beginning and elaborate on this part of the story.

Sugar beets had been grown in Wyo-Braska since the early years of the twentieth century. Most were grown in Scotts Bluff and Morrill Counties of Nebraska as more and more land came under irrigation. At about the same time, beets were being raised in Goshen County, Wyoming; those growers were producing a high-quality crop. In 1920, there were no sugar refineries in the North Platte Valley in Wyoming, and most beets were shipped under contract to the Great Western factories in western Nebraska. Obviously to the movers and shakers in the Torrington area, it seemed that this situation meant that the people in Goshen County and the surrounding area in Wyoming were shipping much of the value added to their crop to Nebraska and not getting the additional benefit they could receive had they had their own local factory.

Most of those involved in the issue realized that railroad access was necessary to provide a factory with a reliable stream of beets during the campaign. At that time, only the Burlington Railroad served the area, and it was on the north side of the North Platte River. The best sugar beet growing area was south of the river in the irrigated lands in the Cherry and Horse Creek areas. Without rail access on the south and fewer available acres for production on the north, they lacked the key pieces to both produce and move the crop from fields to factory in a time of mostly poor, unpaved roads. Rail had been proven as the way to go in Colorado and other places. Rail access was being expanded on both sides of the river in the panhandle. In 1920, the Union Pacific had finally built up the valley on the south side of the river from the east but only as far as Haig, Nebraska. Haig was still about twenty-five miles east of Torrington, and the UP was not quite ready to build west. These handicaps did not stop attempts to recruit a sugar plant for Torrington.

There is no doubt now but that a factory will be built in Torrington ready to take care of the 1921 beet crop. All that remains is the formal signing of contracts as the Holly people have signified their intention of putting a mill at this place.[121]

Details of this industrial triumph for Torrington will likely be ready for publication next week.[122]

Hope springs eternal, and this false alarm is one of several that Torrington would experience in the next few years. (If this story sounds similar to that of the factory at Minatare, it should, because there are many similarities, including the influence of both the Holly Company and Great Western in both affairs.) "The developments of the past week established positively that there will be a factory in Torrington to take care of the 1921 beet crop."[123]

With this first false alarm, the chickens were already being counted by the editor of the newspaper. "OTHER INDUSTRIES TO TORRINGTON. With a sugar factory as good as an assured fact for the coming year, we believe the commercial club is missing a chance in not making an effort to get other industries to locate here."[124]

About a month later, rampant speculation was the way to sell newspapers. "HOLLY SUGAR COMPANY REPRESENTATIVE HERE….Don't anybody get their wires crossed on that beet sugar factory. It's coming and that pretty soon, too."[125]

The speculation, primarily in the *Goshen County Journal* at this time, continued into September and even grew larger.

THREE SUGAR FACTORIES LOOM FOR GOSHEN COUNTY….For several weeks the citizens of Torrington have been on the anxious seat concerning the prospects of a sugar factory here. Nothing definite has developed along that line recently, but The Journal *has accidently stumbled onto some information that has caused us to be stronger of the opinion that there will be a sugar factory here to take care of the 1921 crop than ever before. While we are not at liberty to state our source of information we feel that it is reliable enough to place us in a position to say that we feel assured that there will not only be a sugar factory at Torrington for the 1921 crop but there is a likely hood that there will be built at Lingle and another at Springer for the 1922 crop.*[126]

The speculation appeared to have been contagious, as even the *Scottsbluff Star-Herald* got into the act a short time later.

GOSHEN COUNTY IS YET VERY HOPEFUL....THINKS THAT LOCATION OF
SUGAR FACTORY IS MATTER OF SHORT TIME....When it is considered that
there are three factories operating within a radius of eight miles in Scotts
Bluff county and two more building at Minatare, which will make five
within a radius of sixteen miles, it will readily be seen that one factory in
Goshen county with her one hundred thousand acres of highly productive
irrigated lands will be only a beginning.[127]

It was about this time in 1920 that the cold reality of this first false alarm began to become apparent. In another article in the *Star-Herald* reprinted from the *Lingle Review* came the following:

LINGLE IS PEEVISH ANENT [SIC] *NEW FACTORY-MATTER HAS BLOWN HOT AND*
COLD FOR SOME TIME NOW....A vast unbroken silence has been maintained
by the Holly people as to their proposed sugar factory at Torrington,
although they were supposed to have spoken more than seven sleeps ago....
The Holly company has been flirting with the county for moons so many
that all count has been lost. Two weeks ago the deal was announced as
practically completed for the factory and a positive announcement was due
to arrive within two or three days....This saw almost two weeks ago and
at this time of going to press the silence is so dense that it can be carved
with a spade.[128]

It is with those types of comments that the year 1920 ended for the Torrington sugar factory project. With little information to be found in the press for a while, the project appeared to be placed on the back burner by both the community and the sugar company until early in 1923.

In mid-January 1923, the speculation began anew. A front-page article in the *Telegram* was headlined "ACCORDING TO REPORTS FROM DENVER TORRINGTON IS TO HAVE $1,000,000 SUGAR MILL." The article stated: "Early construction of a $1,000,000 beet sugar refinery at Torrington, Wyo. by the Goshen Sugar Company the first Wyoming sugar beet corporation which will have the moral support of the Lincoln Land company probably the greatest land development concern in the west was announced in Denver, Friday."[129]

Mentioned in the article is the Goshen Sugar Company, which until this point had not apparently been heard of. The exact background and ultimate fate of that entity is very murky. It is mentioned frequently along

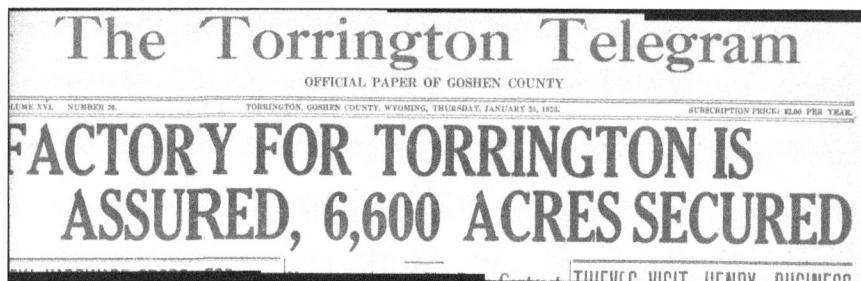

The Torrington Telegram
OFFICIAL PAPER OF GOSHEN COUNTY

FACTORY FOR TORRINGTON IS ASSURED, 6,600 ACRES SECURED

Torrington Telegram headline, January 25, 1923. Torrington Telegram *archives.*

with the Holly Company in the press during 1923. The second round of wild speculation had just begun, as indicated by the headline pictured above.

The story below that headline goes on to detail the assured factory.

> *There has been much rumor afloat in Torrington and the vicinity for some time, and while we have been informed of some things that were taking place we have refrained from mentioned anything in the columns of the Telegram until such time as we could give our readers a definite statement of facts. This has not been possible till the present time.*
>
> *Articles of incorporation have been filed with the Secretary of State, and the new Goshen Sugar concern is fully financed.*[130]

The article goes on: "The efforts of the town of Torrington and the people immediately surrounding the city are about to be realized, for it is an assured fact that if we can sign the necessary acreage, that the new company will build a plant in Torrington in time to grind the 1923 crop of sugar beets grown in Goshen County."[131]

The wild speculation continued in the article.

> *The Great Western officials were in Yoder Thursday looking over the situation for the establishment of a factory for that company for our neighbor....*
>
> *We predict that should they be successful in landing a factory in Yoder this year, it will mean the erection of two sugar refineries in Goshen County.*[132]

One final wild prediction came later in the same front-page article:

> *With the amount of land now under water in this county, there is no reason why Goshen County cannot support at least three 1000 ton sugar plants each year.*[133]

At any rate by Wednesday evening all of this acreage will be signed up, and should we be successful in signing from 7,000 to 8,000 acres of beets it will mean the early construction of the new Goshen factory in Torrington. [134]

In a flurry of new articles up and down the valley, additional news seemed to show up every day. An article in the *Star-Herald* the next day stated that beet acreage was being signed up for the project by the principals involved:

Both Messrs. Pavitt and Roshar had no hesitancy in stating that while the contracts are in the name of the Goshen Hole Sugar company, the real power behind the proposed improvement is the Holly sugar company, but that in order to make it a truly Wyoming enterprise the name of the Goshen Hole Sugar company was chosen and that in practically every respect it will be a Wyoming concern, such as the state had desired for some time. [135]

It is hard to understand how Goshen County residents kept their sanity as the assurances of immediate construction were made over and over for several years. Early 1923 was just another one of those times. A short time later, another front-page story appeared.

SUGAR FACTORY IS TO BE CONSTRUCTED SOON—FULL PARTICULARS AS SOON AS RELEASED.... The Sugar Refinery will positively be built in Torrington this year. [136]

We all feel anxious, and as there is much propaganda going the rounds concerning the new venture we want to set at rest any rumor that is derogatory to the men behind the Goshen Sugar Company. YES WE WILL HAVE A FACTORY IN TORRINGTON. [137]

In an open letter to the beet growers in Goshen County, the president of the Goshen Sugar Company, J.H. McKinnon, stated:

We think it is generally understood throughout the community that satisfactory arrangements have been made for the construction of the factory at Torrington this year but not withstanding this we are advised that certain persons and influences are at work in the community distributing propaganda to the effect that not only will the factory not be built at Torrington this year but that it will never be built. [138]

OFFICIAL PAPER OF GOSHEN COUNTY

SUGAR FACTORY IS ASSURED---
Work To Start Within Ten Days

MRS. ED. C. BEACH DIES AT | U. P. AT CHERRY CREEK WILL | SAYS BEET CONTRACT IS BEST
TORRINGTON HOSPITAL SUNDAY | CONNECT WITH BURLINGTON | IN VIEW LOCAL CONDITIONS.

Torrington Telegram headline, February 22, 1923. Torrington Telegram archives.

The sugar factory will be constructed by the Goshen Sugar Company at Torrington during the year 1923 to handle the 1923 crop of sugar beets.[139]

Another huge headline appeared about a week later, stating for the umpteenth time that it was coming for sure now!

That headline article states that construction of the Torrington factory will start within ten days and that the Union Pacific will build into the area through Cherry Creek and will connect with the Burlington at Torrington. Although it is unspoken, this would have required a railroad bridge over the North Platte to connect the two railroads somewhere in Torrington. The article goes on to elaborate the point that the newspaper writer feels Torrington will soon rival Cheyenne and Casper in size and have limitless potential for growth.

One of the confusing things, among many, is the repeated references to both the Goshen Sugar Company and the Goshen Hole Sugar Company. They are obviously the same entity, but I cannot confirm which is the proper name according to the articles of incorporation. While the exact proposed location of the factory was still up in the air, the company announced that several beet dumps were being established to serve the new factory.

SITE OF FACTORY AND RIGHT-OF-WAY SURVEYED—DUMPS ARE LOCATED— CONSTRUCTION SURE....The Goshen sugar Company has applied for beet dumps as follows, and early construction of them will be undertaken. One dump at Torrington, one at Vaughn, one at Lingle and one at Barnes siding on the Burlington railroad, and one at Huntley, and one at Cottier, and one at a suitable location on Cherry Creek on the Union Pacific Railroad making a total of seven dumps already planned for, and others will be constructed as the need arises.[140]

A few weeks later, in another front-page article, the *Telegram* stated that the Goshen Sugar Company was drawing up plans for the new factory.

> *It is estimated by them that it will take something like 30 days to complete the task of making the plans, maps and blueprints, after which real construction work will begin on coupling the main line of the Burlington with the sugar factory site. Therefore there may be a slight lull in the factory developments, as far as local observations are concerned and the people may be led by this slackening to conclude that the proposition of a factory for Torrington is yet in the distance.*
>
> *We have much to incourage* [sic] *us, in our knowledge that a factory will be built, that active construction will commence at an early date, and that by the end of this year we shall see a factory for this community well on toward completion, and that this alone will make for better times this summer here is an assured fact.*[141]

Also on page one of the same issue is another open letter to the beet growers from George Allen, president of the Goshen Sugar Company. In part, he states:

> *We wish to express our thanks to you for your co-operation in securing the beet acreage for the year 1923 for the Torrington factory....*
>
> *We believe it will be only a few years until the acreage is extended to such an extent that we will not only have one factory but two which will greatly increase the wealth of our county.*[142]

In another wildly speculative front-page article in the same issue is the headline: "GOSHEN COUNTY WYO., HAS VAST UNDEVELOPED RESOURCES—COULD SUPPORT A POPULATION OF 100,000."[143]

To say that that speculation was overly optimistic would be an understatement. Goshen County's population in 1920 was about 8,000. The estimated population almost a century later is just 13,400. Just a little short of the prediction! This type of prediction is not uncommon. Many newspaper people of the time were among the biggest promoters of their communities, and some still are today. That promotion is fine and justified, but in both cases it should be stated in the editorial content of the publication and not as a news story, unless the promotion is from an interview or press release from someone not editing the newspaper.

By mid-April, it had become obvious that there was no way possible for construction of a factory to process the 1923 beet crop. In another *Telegram* article under the headlines of a bright outlook for Goshen Sugar are the following statements:

The construction of the factory here is as certain as day follows night, and by the first of October 1924 the mill will be turning out sugar from Goshen county beets.

Things are moving along nicely, and by the first of July, and possibly before some physical signs of the erection of the plant will have been made manifest.[144]

At the end of May, another article states, "Work on the factory proper, we are told, will begin along about the first of July."[145]

By this time, it was more than obvious that there would not be a Goshen Sugar Company plant to process the 1923 contracted crop. The harvest for the Goshen Sugar Company began in late September. In order to process the crop, an agreement was reached with Great Western to process the beets from south of the river; those from the north side would be processed by Holly at the Sheridan, Wyoming plant. Again, that over-the-top optimism was reflected in an article about the 1923 harvest that quoted E.G. Alliare of Holly Sugar: "Mr. Alliare also stated there was no doubt but what we would have a factory in Torrington which would take care of the 1924 crop."[146]

Thus, as 1923 came to an end, the good folks in Torrington and Goshen County, Wyoming, still did not have that factory that had been assured to them in 1920 and again in 1923!

The year 1924 was fairly quiet regarding speculation as to what was happening with a sugar factory for Torrington. Nothing appears to have been announced for construction for the 1924 crop, and little news seems to have been published in the local press. One article did appear in the *Star-Herald* in early 1924 detailing a possible deal between Holly Sugar and Great Western that would have resulted in GW buying out the interest of Holly in a plant in Worland, Wyoming. According to the article, this would have resulted in the abandonment of future construction plans for a Holly factory at Torrington.

If the offer of the Great Western Sugar Company now pending to purchase the interest of Holly Sugar Company in the Worland factory of the Wyoming Sugar Company is accepted it is understood that a general re-alignment of the sugar industry in Wyoming will result and the sugar factory planned by the Holly Company for Torrington will not be erected.[147]

If the deal with the Great Western company is not completed it is understood the Holly corporation will move its plant at Anaheim, California to Torrington.[148]

There appeared to be little other public activity regarding the Torrington sugar factory during all of 1924 and little information until the fall of 1925. Suddenly, a flurry of news stories began to surface in the press beginning in late September. A story in the *Goshen County Journal* stated: "Holly Program Includes Factory at Torrington. A new sugar factory at Torrington is proposed by the Holly Sugar Company but denial of any intention of building at Minatare at present, in a statement issued by A.E. Carlton, Vice-President of the U.S. Sugar Manufacturers Association of Washington, D.C."[149]

Another article a few days later in the *Gering Courier* points to the same outcome. In early October, an article in the *Goshen County Journal* announced that Great Western would restart construction of the mill at Minatare and that it intended another factory in Nebraska on the Union Pacific west of Gering. Another article published the same day states: "The Holly Sugar Company has made a step toward construction of its sugar factory at Torrington. The mechanical architect was in Torrington the first of the week and surveyed the tract which the sugar company owns south of Torrington and located the tract where the factory will be erected....Rumor has it that excavating will start soon."[150]

Another hint of a possible railroad bridge across the river is contained later in the article. "The survey for the railroad across the Platte River from Torrington down to the factory is also completed. This connects the Burlington with the factory so that the fine beets, which are produced on the north side of the river, can be taken to the Holly plant to be turned into sugar."[151]

Another example of unbridled optimism is contained mid-article: "Yoder and La Grange are both in line for a factory in the near future."[152]

The press was starting to suggest a sugar war between Holly and Great Western, as each hinted at plans to expand into each other's traditional growers' territory. Holly hinted of construction of a mill on the front range of Colorado (traditional Great Western territory) as retaliation for the planned new GW factory in western Scotts Bluff County south of the river. At this point, everyone was still waiting for a formal announcement of Holly starting construction, but everything appeared to be moving that way without that formal announcement. In another article in early October, A.E. Carlton, Holly Sugar's president, was interviewed. "INTERVIEW BY PRESIDENT A.E. CARLTON ASSURES WORK WILL START IMMEDIATELY ON HOLLY FACTORY AT TORRINGTON. The site south of Torrington has been bought and paid for and the necessary surveys and factory plans are completed."[153]

Later in the interview is another hint of a planned railroad bridge connection over the Platte to the Burlington on the north side. "The location of the factory at the site selected means the extension of both railroads to the factory site and the construction of a railroad bridge across the North Platte River."[154]

An editorial in the same issue of the *Telegram* again makes plain the expected railroad expansions to serve the new factory. "From statements made by reliable authorities in connection with the building of the factory, a railroad track will be built from the Burlington line across the river to the factory site, the railroad bridge to be just seven hundred feet west of the highway bridge."[155]

One thing missing from all the discussion of the coming Torrington factory is the Goshen Sugar Company. It apparently disappeared during the roughly eighteen months of quiet activities and there now was no doubt that Holly was the main player in this development. The sugar war continued between the two principles as Great Western announced in mid-October that its new mill would be built at Lyman, Nebraska, just a short distance east of Torrington and right on the Nebraska/Wyoming state line. This was seen as a threat to Holly's control over the beet-raising lands in the Goshen Hole area just west of Lyman on the expanding Union Pacific right-of-way.

A statement made in the *Telegram* in mid-October is really a little hard to believe based on the track record of the press on this issue in the previous few years in question.

> *There are many rumors about different moves being made but the Telegram proposes to print nothing except official news from the offices of the company. There has been much street talk about the moves of both the Holly and the Great Western but nothing definite has come to the Telegram. The activities of the representatives of both companies have led to much speculation as to what the outcome of this little sugar war will be.*[156]

The statement is somewhat comical, based on the history of wild speculation that had taken place regarding the Torrington factory in the preceding years and cited several times in this chapter. At this point in time, it did seem like the efforts for a Torrington mill were finally nearing fruition. The sugar war was continuing as Holly announced in late November that it too would build a factory at Minatare, in direct competition with Great Western. Much of that story has been covered in an earlier chapter but is mentioned again here to put it in context with what was going on at the same time.

The anti-speculation pledge from the *Telegram* was apparently not shared by the *Goshen County Journal*, as a couple of weeks later, another article based on rumors was in print.

> *More Sugar Factories for N.P. Valley. Latest rumors regarding additional sugar factories to be built in this part of Nebraska include one at Bridgeport and one in the Lodge Pole Valley near Kimball. And both seem to have some semblance of foundation as officers of the Utah Sugar Company and the Holly Company have been in these places looking over ground and conferring with the businessmen regarding erection of factories.* [157]

> *President Carlton of the Holly Company and engineers of that company, with the agent of the Lincoln Land Company have also been in Bridgeport, and gave almost positive assurance that a factory of the Holly people would be built there in 1927.* [158]

As all the activities of the local sugar war were going on, international sugar prices were collapsing. A bumper crop of cane sugar was flooding the market and lowering prices for producers. Great Western announced an immediate reduction of fifty cents per one hundred pounds of sugar. The retail price reached the lowest level it had seen in many years. This increased competition and reduced tariff protection for the domestic sugar producers did not bode well for the industry, but it apparently was not yet recognized, as factory construction and beet production continued to expand.

As 1925 neared its end, construction had still not started on the plant. As had been the case so many times in the past, people in the area were probably still concerned that this might be another false alarm. Despite all the assurances, they had to be waiting for Holly to break ground and start pouring foundations for the buildings.

As November neared its end, Holly secured financing for the two mills at Torrington and Minatare and created another company, the Wyoming-Nebraska Sugar Company, as a subsidiary. I can only assume that the creation of this entity may have had some tax or financing advantages, even though it would operate as a wholly owned subsidiary of Holly.

At this same time, the sugar war between the companies was leading to many questions from growers, who were increasingly unhappy with Great Western's contract price offer. Holly was offering more, and growers were asking why.

As an interesting side story to the sugar war, it became apparent that it was affecting other industries outside of sugar production. In early December, a newspaper article stated the following:

> Another industry hard hit by sugar price war. Another industry that is temporarily paralyzed by the sugar price war is the honey industry. Honey prices have dropped to a much lower figure than ever heard of before in the cities and as a result the moving of honey is practically at a standstill at the present. Thus it is seen how a sugar company starting a price war can damage several lines of industry.[159]

As these activities were going on, Union Pacific filed notice to extend its track the four miles from Cottier in the Cherry Creek area to South Torrington to serve the new Holly factory that was expected soon. Things were moving in the direction of fulfilling the long dreamed of result of a sugar factory in Torrington, but as 1925 drew to a close, ground had still not been broken for the mill there.

As the sun rose on Torrington on January 21, 1926, it began to appear that the news regarding the Torrington sugar factory was finally about to become reality. A front-page article in the *Telegram* quoted H.A. Benning, Holly general manager in the area, stating that Holly would build a two-thousand-ton factory in Torrington and that plans for a Holly factory in Minatare, Nebraska, had been abandoned as an economic waste, as there was probably insufficient beet production in the immediate area there to support two factories. The article elaborates by stating that the original plans for Torrington's factory had been for a 1,200-ton capacity, but with the abandonment of their idea for a Minatare mill, the production capacity for the new mill in Goshen County would be increased to the previously mentioned two thousand tons. The construction plan included dismantling and moving the equipment from a Holly plant in Huntington Beach, California. The California plant had been determined to have insufficient production to be economically viable. Additional new equipment was promised to fill in any deficiencies from the California material.

These actions were reviewed in an editorial the next week.

> The latest move means that the sugar war is over. The companies will no longer fight over territory but will respect each other's priority.[160]

It would appear that this move means that the Great Western will keep out of Wyoming territory and the Holly will stay out of Nebraska territory and each company will be unhampered in developing its respective potential beet territory.[161]

The long-awaited construction of the mill finally started in early February 1926 with the pouring of the footings for the warehouse on the eighth. A 250-foot-tall smokestack was part of the planned factory, and it too started about the same time. The completion of the warehouse would provide a space to safely store the equipment coming from the California plant as well as other materials that might be damaged by exposure to the weather. "The first carload of steel brought in on newly laid Union Pacific rails arrived Wednesday February 24, 1926."[162]

The factory was being built by two shifts of over one hundred workers total. By mid-April, more than 150 cars of material and machinery had been delivered to the site by the Union Pacific.

Wagons at the Holly construction site in Torrington, 1926. *Courtesy Homesteaders Museum, Torrington, Wyoming.*

A labor dispute between some of the workers and the contractor was quickly settled when the Carpenters Union tried to organize them; about twenty-five men who had joined were promptly fired, as the contractor chose to negotiate with individual workers and not a group. While not regarded as a fair labor practice today, it was not uncommon at the time. After the concrete work was completed, the night shift, which had been involved with the day shift in continuously pouring concrete, was laid off. Their idle time did not last long; many were rehired in short order. In mid-April, there were about three hundred men working on the construction of the factory.

By midsummer, over seven hundred men were employed at the site. It was announced that they would test-run the plant by mid-September and, if all went well, begin receiving beets in early October. Other businessmen in the Torrington area were beginning to benefit from the plant's operation as well.

> With the newly built factory came some fairly advanced ideas. Clyde Smith, owner of Smith's Drug Store, secured the concession from Holly to operate a lunch stand in the factory building. The lunch stand was to give 24 hour service and hot food.[163]

> L.H. Bump, owner of Bump Motor Company, sold Holly 24 Chevrolet trucks to be delivered in one shipment.[164]

Top: Twenty-four Chevy trucks sold to Holly at Torrington by Bump Motors in late 1926. Star-Herald *photo, February 11, 2017.*

This page, bottom: Holly Sugar plant at Torrington, construction, 1926. *Courtesy Homesteaders Museum, Torrington, Wyoming.*

Mr. Bump apparently had a satisfied customer in Holly; it is documented in local papers that he sold twenty-five more in 1927 and fifty in August 1928!

The benefits of the new factory were huge. In an August article, the amount of beets grown south of the river in recent years was documented.

It will be recalled that in 1923 there were only 19 cars of sugar beets raised south of the river. This increased in 1924 to 800 cars. In 1925 to 1500 cars and in 1926 the total will run over 3000.[165]

Sugar beets are coming in great trucks and railroad cars. Big piles of beets that stand out like ranges of the Rockies surround the factory. To those not familiar with the work it would appear that all the beets in the world are piled up in the yards, but when it is remembered that 2,000 tons of beets are handled daily and that 175,000 tons of beets have been produced in this district this year, for the Holly Sugar Corporation, an idea of the quantity required is obtained.[166]

As with any heavy industry, factory work can be dangerous, and sugar factory work was no different. At this time, the factories were a maze of gears and belts and other dangerous machinery. A momentary lapse of concentration could prove devastating to a worker. Such an incident occurred a few months after the plant opened. A horrific headline in a small front-page article in early December documents such an incident.

Piling beets at the Holly plant in Torrington, circa 1930. Star-Herald *photo, February 11, 2017.*

HEAD COMPLETELY SEVERED FROM BODY—*Terrible death meets sugar factory employee....Death in a horrible form overtook Fred Manning last Sunday afternoon when he was drawn into the cogs of the machinery at which he was working and his head completely severed from his body at the new sugar factory at Torrington....This is the first fatality at the new mill.*[167]

The factory was finally complete and in full operation. It was considered state of the art at the time and was one of the larger factories in the nation. Like the Great Western plants in Scottsbluff and some other locations, feedlots were located directly adjacent to the west to utilize some of the beet pulp for livestock feed with little transportation cost.

Like many industries. it experienced labor shortages during the Second World War. Local businesses were urged to assign one of their employees

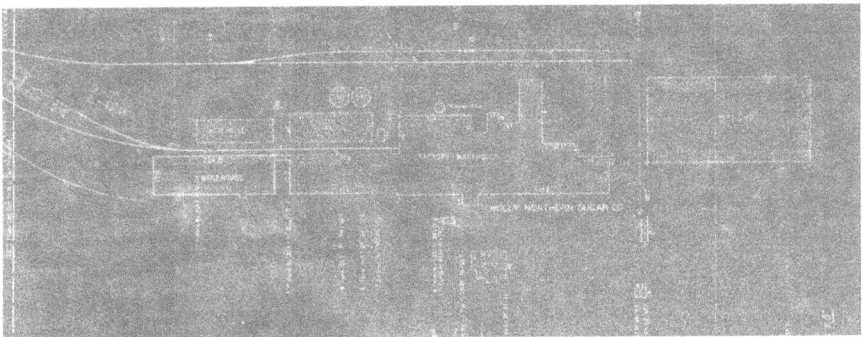

Top: Holly plant after completion, late 1920s. *Courtesy Homesteaders Museum, Torrington, Wyoming.*

Bottom: Holly Sugar Torrington site plan, 1928. *Union Pacific line map. Author's collection.*

Aerial view of Holly Torrington sugar factory showing feedlots, circa 1930. *Courtesy Homesteaders Museum, Torrington, Wyoming.*

Holly Sugar factory at Torrington, Wyoming, June 2019. *Photo by the author.*

to harvesting beets in the field in 1944, and schools were closed in Veteran, Huntley and Hawk Springs to help with the harvest. Additional labor was provided by voluntary Japanese American workers from the Heart Mountain Relocation Camp near Cody.

The Torrington Holly plant would operate successfully for almost a century.

> *The industry survived wars and weather, but ran into an almost insurmountable financial hurdle in the 1970s and '80s. Worldwide conditions, along with disastrous management practices by parent companies nearly closed the Torrington operations in the early 1980s. It labored through the next two decades, but the arrival of the 21ˢᵗ century brought too much upheaval for the Goshen County operation to continue.*
>
> *In 2001, Holly managed to reach its 75ᵗʰ anniversary of production in Torrington before it fell victim to financial hardships of the parent company.*
>
> *An effort by area producers to purchase the Goshen County business failed and in 2002 the facility was purchased by American Crystal which leased it to Western Sugar Cooperative, the new grower-owned Western Sugar.*[168]

Western Sugar continued to process beets at the factory, but the reprieve was short-lived. After aborted attempts to close the factory in 2016 and 2017, Western Sugar finally announced that the 2018 campaign would be the last one for processing. Like some of the other Western Sugar factories in the valley, it would be used primarily for sugar storage in the future, as all North Platte Valley processing would be finally consolidated at the updated Scottsbluff mill. The repeated efforts and eventual success by the community to obtain a sugar factory in the 1920s finally came to an end a century later.

6

FACTORIES THAT MIGHT HAVE BEEN
BUT NEVER WERE

I t became obvious in my several years of research on the subject of this book
that in the North Platte Valley (and perhaps other places) in the period
from about 1910 to 1930, having a sugar factory in your community was
considered the golden goose that would lay golden eggs for the rest of the
community. Rumors circulated widely during that time in the area that, with
various degrees of certainty, a factory was being considered for each of the
hopeful communities.

During this period, many communities were supposedly on the to-be-
built list. Much of this speculation may have been wishful thinking on the
part of newspaper editors hoping to sell more newspapers with the latest
rumor that the sugar mill was coming any day now. For the most part, it
was wishful thinking.

Some of the communities mentioned in earlier parts of this book that were
at least supposedly on track for a factory included Lingle, Yoder, Springer
and La Grange in Wyoming and Bridgeport, the Lodge Pole Valley near
Kimball, Haig and Lewellen in Nebraska.

*Lewellen, at Least Is Still Optimistic—Booster Club of that Village
appoints committee to try to get Sugar Factory There—Despite the rather
discouraging situation further up the valley, the farmers of the Lewellen
neighborhood are planning a further agitation for a sugar factory, evidently
believing that the present condition is but temporary and that brighter days
are eventfully in store for the industry.*[169]

To place that article in context, this announcement would have occurred only a few days after Great Western Sugar suspended construction on its Minatare plant due to the condition of the sugar market at that time. Hope springs eternal, even in the face of bad news.

Of those just listed, only Bridgeport progressed slightly past the rumor stage. At that, maybe it was only rumors and wild speculation as well.

BRIDGEPORT, NEBRASKA

As early as the spring of 1902, some people in the Bridgeport area had determined that the soil in the area was perfect for growing sugar beets. It was speculated that it would take a couple of years of production of beets (these would have to be shipped elsewhere for processing) to show that sufficient tonnage could come from the surrounding area. The people of Bridgeport and the nearby communities would need to work together to convince people, or a company, to invest the million or so dollars it would take to build one there. Nothing happened at that time.

Speculation about a factory to be located in Bridgeport became more intense in the fall of 1925, after several mills had been built farther up the valley beginning in 1909 at Scottsbluff.

> *More Sugar Factories for the N.P. Valley—Latest rumors regarding additional sugar factories to be built in this part of Nebraska include one in Bridgeport and in the Lodge Pole Valley near Kimball. And both seem to have some semblance of foundation as officers of the Utah Sugar company and the Holly Company have been in these places looking over the ground and conferring with the business men regarding erection of factories.*[170]

> *President Carlton of the Holly company and engineers of that company with the agent of the Lincoln Land company have also been in Bridgeport, and gave almost positive assurance that a factory of the Holly people would be built there in 1927, declaring that the building campaign for 1926 was filled, with the factory at Torrington, Wyo. and Minatare, which had practically been agreed upon.*[171]

That promise from Holly disappeared rather quickly, probably caused by the settlement of the sugar war and the unofficial agreements for the

Beet dump at Bridgeport, circa 1924. *Courtesy Oregon Trail Museum, Bridgeport, Nebraska.*

two companies to keep out of each other's territory. Nothing apparently transpired of Bridgeport's quest for a factory until midsummer 1927. Suddenly, the project seemed to take off very quickly. Or so it seemed, this time with a totally independent sugar company.

ACTIVE PLANS GET UNDER WAY TO ERECT SUGAR PLANT IMMEDIATELY AT BRIDGEPORT—COMPANY FORMED—Plans for the erection of a sugar factory at Bridgeport are proceeding with full speed the past few days.—A pre-organization outline of the plans for the formation of a company to be known as the North Platte Valley Sugar Company has been prepared and is being mailed out to possible interested parties in the territory.—The outline as mailed out by the committee states in part: The organization committee of the proposed North Platte Valley Sugar Company has negotiations underway for securing the complete sugar factory plant of the Peoples Sugar Company in Utah. The plant has been unsuccessful on account of short beet crops with which to operate.[172]

The factory would have slicing capacity of about 1,200 tons, which would be comparable with the other North Platte Valley plants except for Scottsbluff, which is larger. Like Minatare and Torrington before them, the wild speculation on the newspapers' front pages began.

The plant, owned by the Peoples Sugar Company of Maroni, Utah, was apparently for sale, cheap! According to the press, it could be purchased for

BRIDGEPORT, MORRILL COUNTY, NEBRASKA, AUGUST 4, 1927

R. O. CANADAY REPORTS BACK ON UTAH INVESTIGATION AND FOUND EVERYTHING TO BE BETTER THAN WAS AT FIRST TOLD

Plant Equipped With Sugar Industry's Newest Machinery Used but to the Equivalent of Two Compaigns

OPTIONS ENABLE BRIDGEPORT TO BUY MIL- LION DOLLAR PLANT AT 50¢ ON THE DOLLAR

Plans Call for Organization $1,500,000 Sugar Company to Be Known as "The North Platte Valley Sugar Company, Bridgeport."

Headline of the *Bridgeport News-Blade*, August 4, 1927. *Courtesy* Bridgeport News-Blade *Archives.*

half of what it was worth. R.O. Canaday, an attorney from Bridgeport, had journeyed to Utah to inspect the machinery of the potential purchase. "He failed to find one feature that was not more than as represented by the Utah men who have been in Bridgeport for the last few weeks in the interests of the proposed company."[173]

The Utah Company would be acquired for fifty cents on the dollar, and that money would be given to the current owners in the form of stock in the new North Platte Valley Sugar Company. The company would be governed by a seven-member board of directors, three of whom will be owners of the current Utah plant. Additional stock would be sold locally at a cost of ten dollars per share. A meeting of people interested in the proposal was called for Friday night, August 5, at the Miller Opera House.

Canaday and others, including the mayor of Bridgeport, Gus Weisbach, were signers of a large ad in the same issue of the *News-Blade*. In the promotional ad, the plan is detailed. "The Plan....It is proposed to organize a corporation to be known as The North Platte Valley Sugar Co., capitalized at $1,500,000. $150,000 worth of stock is to be subscribed here in the valley and the balance will go to pay for machinery, building, and cash capitol to operate the factory with when started."[174]

The ad concludes with the reassuring statement, "Bridgeport's Sugar Mill Plans Will Stand the Most Rigid Investigation."[175]

The following week, another bold headline appeared in the *News-Blade*: "Bridgeport's sugar factory now seems assured according to information given out to those men who have the matter in hand. Committees are working hard, subscriptions are coming in fast and several large subscriptions have helped to swell the total."[176]

Headline of the *Bridgeport News-Blade*, August 11, 1927. *Courtesy* Bridgeport News-Blade *Archives*.

One interesting feature of the stock sale is a time payment plan to pay for stock purchases. Pay for it in ten easy payments, said the promoters. A representative of the Wrigley chewing gum company from Chicago, principle stock owners in the Gunnison Sugar Company, was in attendance. W. Harvey Ross, president of the Gunnison Company, was in favor of the new company and reassured people that it almost could not fail due to the quality of the equipment, the availability of beets in the valley and the reputation of N.G. Stringham, who apparently would run the plant. Additional promotional letters followed in the same issue on page two, urging people to buy stock in the company. One of the key proposals of the new mill is that the growers and the company would have a fifty-fifty split on any profits from the beets they would grow for the factory.

In a *Star-Herald* article in mid-October, growers in the area committed to supply the proposed factory with beets for the 1928 harvest season.

> *Citizens of Bridgeport and the surrounding territory feel assured that a sugar factory will be erected there within a short time and be ready for the next season's output of beets. The feeling of assurance is based in part on the action of the Cooperative Beet Growers Association, when its board of directors voted at a recent meeting to guarantee the company ten thousand acres of beets for the slicing at Bridgeport. The resolution, which carries the guarantee, provides that the agreement shall be in effect after the association has made full investigation of the sugar company, known as the North Platte Valley Sugar Company, relative to its ability to carry out contracts which will be entered into with the growers.*[177]

No word was given out by the association as to when its investigation of the project will be complete, and when its agreement to deliver beets will be made final.[178]

It appears, based on the newspaper article just cited, that the beet growers were beginning to have a little skepticism of the project, based on the need for an investigation by them before committing to any contracts for supplying beets.

In an article in the *News-Blade* a week before the above referenced *Star-herald* article, the proposal was still promoted in the headline and article.

SUGAR MILL SEEMS NEAR CONSUMATION....Bridgeport's sugar mill is not by any means a dead issue. Quite the contrary is true.[179]

It is understood that in the event the investigation [referenced in the previous *Star-Herald* article] *is not started within the ten day period, the contract for the delivery of the beets is to become in full force and effect. Just who will be delegated to make the investigation it was not determined but it is expected that one of the directors* [of the beet growers association] *will make a trip to Salt Lake City at once and inquire into the matter.*[180]

A great deal of additional research has turned up little more information about the North Platte Valley Sugar Company in the local media.

I was able to determine that the Peoples Sugar Company of Moroni, Utah, which closed in 1925, was indeed sold during 1928. It went to Toppenish, Washington, however, not to Bridgeport, Nebraska.

ANOTHER POSSIBLE FACTORY

In the late winter and early spring of 1928, still another possible factory was being discussed. This one would have been a cooperative factory, owned by the growers, at a specific site in the valley never mentioned. At a meeting of the Cooperative Beet Growers Association in Scottsbluff on February 22, the growers decided to build their own plant for the 1928 crop after failing to reach a satisfactory beet contract agreement with Great Western. It was determined at the meeting that it would take $1,000,000 to build a new mill, and they had pledges of $100,000 on the first night.

The decision to erect a cooperative mill has been forced upon the growers by the recent price controversy with the company. Two years ago the Great Western advanced the guaranteed price for beets to $8.00 per ton, last year the company placed a tariff clause in the contract which meant a possible $7.00 for beets.[181]

The board has the assurance from reliable source that the machinery can be furnished and the factory completed in time to grind the 1928 crop.[182]

A few weeks later, the controversy continued. At another meeting on April 4, the growers were being urged to grow alternate crops for 1928 if the new mill could not be ready for 1928 and not to surrender to Great Western's offer of seven dollars per ton.

Eben Warner assured the audience that it was a certainty that a cooperative sugar factory would be erected in the valley and that the coming week would determine whether it would be ready for the 1928 slicing campaign, or the 1929 campaign. Sufficient funds are already on hand in sufficient amount to make possible the beginning of construction at once, he stated. It is still possible that a factory can be ready for this year's crop, Mr. Warner declared.[183]

As was the case so many times in the valley during this decade, this was not to be. Trying to build a plant to be fully operational at an as yet to be determined site in a short five months was at best an unlikely proposition. Even Great Western, with all its construction experience, completed its fastest mill construction at Lyman in about fifteen months from announcement of its building to the first beet slicing. Great Western already had a site chosen when it announced the mill as well. I cannot find any more information about this co-op plant, and nothing ever was built so far as I can determine. Another wishful dream dashed.

It was in this period that the sugar factory building boom of the last twenty years in the North Platte Valley was coming to an end. The Lyman Great Western plant was the last one completed in the valley in 1927. Although speculation of other mills probably continued after that time, the declining market for domestically produced sugar, increased foreign competition and ongoing disputes between the sugar companies and the growers probably put an end to any further construction. The boom was coming to an end.

THE RAILROADS AND THE BEET SPURS

The Chicago, Burlington and Quincy Railroad (CB&Q), commonly referred to as the Burlington, arrived in Alliance, Nebraska, in 1889. A predecessor of the Burlington was actually built into Alliance as the Nebraska, Wyoming and Western (NW&W). The Burlington absorbed the NW&W in about 1908 and would operate in western Nebraska under the Burlington name alone until the merger creating the Burlington Northern in 1970.

The Burlington proceeded to continue west with a line toward the Wyoming coal fields in the 1890s. Another line proceeded south toward Brush, Colorado, splitting again at Northport. At that point, a line continued south through Bridgeport and another west up the North Platte Valley toward Torrington. This line would play an important part in the history of the early sugar beet industry in the valley. The line arrived in Scottsbluff in 1900, beating the Union Pacific's promised construction west up the valley by over a decade. This difference in construction eras is still obvious today, as Scottsbluff is roughly twice the size of Gering, in part due to the decade head start of a railroad's arrival.

As the sugar industry began to be established in the valley in the first decade of the twentieth century, the Burlington would play an integral part in its establishment, expansion and success. Before the Scottsbluff factory was opened, some beets were raised in the Scottsbluff and Mitchell areas and were shipped to Sterling, Colorado, for processing on the Burlington. As mentioned in the earlier chapter on the Scottsbluff factory, loading the beets into railcars at that time was a real problem, since there were no organized beet dumps yet in 1907–8. With the opening of the Scottsbluff factory in 1910, it became obvious that in order to facilitate prompt arrival of the crop to the factory, beet dumps would need to be established, as Great Western had done already in Colorado. Beet dumps on the Burlington main line up the valley would eventually be established at Vanve on the Alliance line north of Northport; then west on the line at De Graw, Bridgeport, Atkins, Prinz, Bayard and Bradley in Morrill County; Snell, Minatare, Winters, Scottsbluff, Covert, Mitchell, Toohey, Morrill and Henry in Scotts Bluff Counties in Nebraska; and at Torrington, Vaughn, Lingle and Barnes in Goshen County, Wyoming. In many cases, the dumps were named after the town where they were located or for the landowner of the property where the dump was established.

As the industry became established in the valley and more growers were raising beets, it became painfully obvious that the position of the dumps only along the established right-of-way was not adequate. Roads were virtually nonexistent in most of the area, and many were little more than dirt wagon trails that quickly became muddy quagmires when the weather failed to cooperate at harvest time. Early October rains or early winter snows quickly made getting the harvested beets to the dump or the factory almost impossible. When the beets didn't arrive when needed, the factories were inefficient in refining without their main material. "To serve these factories, Edmund Simmons, GW's Nebraska District general manager envisioned the idea of short spur lines, each about six miles long, running at right angles to the existing main lines and reaching into the heart of beet-growing country."[184]

It was at first a hard sell to convince both the Burlington and Great Western Sugar to invest the approximately $40,000 per mile that it would take to construct these proposed spurs. In order to get it done, the North Platte Valley Railway was created in late 1919. I'll go into more detail about the NPV Railway a little later.

Railroads in the early twentieth century were still considered vital to the economic success of a town. One of the towns off the beaten path in Banner County was Harrisburg. Many there had pursued a railroad into the county for a number of years. Their hopes were dashed by the UP in 1928, when its extension from Creighton, Wyoming, to the UP transcontinental main line near Egbert, Wyoming, missed the west side of Banner County by a few miles. A second blow was dealt by the Burlington in late 1928, when its consideration of a line west from the Bridgeport area along Pumpkin Creek

Burlington SD-9 locomotive brings loaded beet hoppers off the Bayard-Carlson spur, circa 1966. *Henderson Collection at Legacy of the Plains Museum, Gering, Nebraska.*

Showing the difficulties of harvesting and transporting beets before the transport by rail, a loaded beet wagon lies stuck in the mud on the left while another has been turned into a sleigh to move across the muddy, partly frozen field. *Courtesy Homesteaders Museum, Torrington, Wyoming.*

to the Harrisburg area failed to materialize. Officials from the Burlington and from the area toured the proposed route in mid-August 1928. It was speculated that there would be a considerable amount of agricultural traffic that would utilize the proposed line for shipment of wheat, livestock and possibly even sugar beets. Since the line was never built, it appears that the speculation of traffic to be generated did not come up to the expectations of the railroad officials. The Burlington would play a very important part in the North Platte Valley sugar industry for over half a century and still has some traffic from the Scottsbluff plant today, primarily consisting of bulk sugar and incoming loads of coke and limestone. Sugar beets themselves are no longer part of that traffic, as all of them are brought to the factory by truck.

The next critical railroad-related part of this story is the North Platte Valley Railway.

> *In order to build the needed spurs, GW incorporated the North Platte Valley Railway on Dec. 19, 1919. Constructed in 1920 by this company were the following: Scottsbluff-Mintel, 13.52 miles; Mitchell-Porter 10.14 miles and from the railhead of CB&Q's 4.52 mile (sugar beet) spur from Bayard to Tony, on to Everett 9.43 miles. NPV built a two-mile extension of the Bayard spur in 1924 from Everett to Carlson. The entire NPV property was leased to CB&Q on Feb. 7, 1920. In 1926, CB&Q constructed a 6.37 mile spur from Prinz to Perrin. This made a total of four beet spurs operated by the Burlington, which in 1937 purchased the NPV property.*[185]

According to the articles of incorporation and board meeting minutes, article five established that the railroad would exist for a term of fifty years plus renewal at that time if needed. The railroad founders were the previously mentioned Edmund Simmons, Adolphus Ginn, August Heldt, Carey Campbell and Edwin Clay. The incorporation was granted on January 3, 1920, for a fee of $876.10.

As of February 4, 1920, there were 1,757 shares of stock issued at a value of $100 per share. Great Western Sugar owned 1,750 of the shares; the other 7 were owned by individual investors. There was considerable turnover on the board of directors in the first few years of the railway's existence. Over the years, additional stock was issued and sold. The railroad operation appears to have been fairly profitable, as it shows $55,421.67 in surplus income on March 31, 1926. (That is the equivalent of about $782,000 in 2017 dollars.) Sometime during the 1928–29 year, the CB&Q

A crane lays rail on the Bayard-Perrin "Red Willow" beet spur (the last one built in the valley), August 14, 1926. *Photo licensed from Nebraska State Historical Society.*

took control of the railroad with the purchase of 11,850 shares of stock. It continued to be profitable, declaring surplus income every year through 1936, when it showed a profit of $73,460 ($1.3 million in 2017 dollars). On March 24, 1937, the shareholders, now totally dominated by the Burlington railroad, voted unanimously to sell said railway to the Burlington. At a final meeting held on January 5, 1938, the board unanimously voted to dissolve the corporation and transfer all assets to the Burlington.

It has been nearly impossible to find any photographs of operations by the CB&Q on the NPV Rwy. branches.

The North Platte Valley branches near Scottsbluff were always worked at night, so photos there are virtually non-existent.[186]

The North Platte Valley during sugar beet campaigns ran a raft of trains: a Scottsbluff-Mitchell switcher which went up a long spur; a Scottsbluff-Lingle turnaround; a Scottsbluff Hill job; a Bayard spur and factory switcher; and a daily Alliance-Scottsbluff beet run. These assignments handled beets and beet products only, plus sugar factory coal.[187]

It appears from documents I have found that the Burlington actually constructed the first part of the Bayard west spur beginning in 1917. There was a great deal of speculation in the press in late 1919 that the Bayard west line would be extended much farther west.

> *As the tentative survey now stands the extension begins at the end of the present spur northwest of Bayard and continues northwest some five miles north of Minatare, connecting once more with the main line in this city and swinging away through the Sunflower neighborhood missing Mitchell to the north about two or three miles, and about the same distance north of Morrill, crossing the Scottsbluff-Sioux county line on the dividing line between ranges 56 and 57.*[188]

Due to an apparent problem with securing land right-of-way for this proposed extension, it never happened as described in the article. If you look at the map of the three western spurs on the north side, you will note that much of the area described in the extension was eventually served by the North Platte Valley Railway, not in a continuous branch line paralleling the Burlington main up the valley but in the right-angle spurs proposed by GW's Simmons.

Progress on the spurs was reported almost monthly in issues of the *Sugar Press*:

> *All departments of the North Platte Valley Railway Company at Scottsbluff are very busily engaged in getting everything ready to commence the hauling of beets by October 1st.*[189]

> *It is quite a sensation to see locomotives running north from the factory site. It speaks well for those in charge of the affairs of the North Platte Valley Railway Company to have the work so well advanced at this time.*[190]

> *Work trains are daily seen on the three spurs of the North Platte Valley railway finishing the ballasting of the track, and in ten days beets will be rolling in from the newly opened beet sections. Mr. Vandemore, the railway agent, is too busy to take a vacation.*[191]

Burlington Railroad Agricultural promotional map showing the irrigated crop land in the North Platte Valley and the beet spurs built to service it. *1927 Chicago, Burlington & Quincy Railroad brochure map. Author's collection.*

The building of the three spurs of the North Platte Valley Railroad with three new dumps on each spur has eliminated much of the congestion of teams, and especially at the Scottsbluff factory dump.[192]

Each of the spurs is interesting in their own right. Let's look at them one at a time. We'll begin with that original spur running west from Bayard, the start of which was made by the Burlington. It built a total of 7.14 miles to the north and west from the west side of the Bayard factory in 1917. This construction included the beet dumps at Becker at 2.52 miles, Craft at 4.55 miles, both in Morrill County, and Tony at 7.14 miles in Scotts Bluff County. In 1920, the NPV Railway resumed construction west and built the dumps at Clouse at 9.47 miles, Baxter at 11.85 miles and Carlson at 14.37 miles. The branch was again extended in 1924 to Roberts at 15.58 miles and to the end at Everett at 16.37 miles from the beginning of the spur at the Burlington main line by the Bayard factory. This was by far the longest of the North Platte Valley spurs when it was completed, extending to a point just east of what would eventually become the Scotts Bluff County airport. This line operated at its full length until 1941, at which time the .41 mile of line west of Roberts was abandoned. Operations on the remainder of the line continued for the next twenty-five years until 1966, when the 3.21 miles west of Baxter was retired. The shrinkage continued in 1968, when the next 2.95 miles were abandoned west of Clouse. The remainder of the spur met its final fate in the summer of 1972.

Two of the remaining three NPV Railway spurs were built in 1920. The next one we will look at is the Scottsbluff spur. The Scottsbluff-Mintel spur began just east of the Scottsbluff mill. It proceeded north-northeast for 4.38 miles, at which point the Trout beet dump was established. Continuing on another 2.89 miles was the James beet dump.

Mintle Beet Dump six miles north of Scottsbluff which contains twenty thousand tons of be

The line took a sharp north-northwesterly turn at that point, moving through the Lake Alice school area for another 2.34 miles where the Thomas dump was sited. Moving farther along 1.47 miles was the Marlin dump, which ceased operation after a few years. Continuing on for an additional 2.14 miles was the Mintel dump, near the physical end of the line. This line was abandoned almost in its entirety in the summer of 1974 except for the first 2.25 miles, which at that time served two small industries.

The Mitchell spur begins on the west side of the factory there and goes north and then northwest. It begins with the first dump at Doyle, 3.33 miles from the factory. Again, this dump operated for only a few years, but those are not identified. Moving on to the northwest, 2.11 miles up the line was the

Left: Beet Harvest Satur Farm Lake Alice community near James Beet Dump, 1950s. *Satur family photo*.

Below: Panoramic view of the Mintel beet dump showing a huge pile of beets waiting loading and transport by rail to the Scottsbluff factory, circa mid-1920s. *O.W. Simmons photo, legacy of the Plains Museum collection*.

make sixty thousand bags of sugar   Photo by O. W. Simmons

Redus dump. Continuing on in the same direction and crossing the county line from Scotts Bluff into Sioux County we would have found the Scoville dump, 2.58 miles farther up the line. Again, this dump did not operate for the full duration of the line. Next up the line would have been the Roach dump, another 1.03 miles along. Completing the trip on this spur would have been the Porter dump, located .95 mile farther. Porter may have been unique in the area, as it had a wye for turning the locomotives and a U-shaped hi line trestle. This line was abandoned west of Roach in 1942. The remainder met its final fate again in the summer of 1972.

One more spur was built by the NPV in 1926. This one connected with the Burlington main line about 4.0 miles east of the Bayard factory, just east of the Prinz beet dump. It proceeded north to the Piper beet dump 2.36 miles and then on to the Perrin Dump 3.79 miles farther north. This line opened up the Red Willow Creek area for the growing of beets. This line operated for forty-two years, being abandoned in 1968.

This was the extent of the construction and operation of the beet spurs from the North Platte Valley Railway and the Burlington. Additional beet spurs were built on the south side of the North Platte River by the Union Pacific.

Dump at either Porter or Roach (not identified) on the Mitchell beet spur. The dump included a wye to turn the locomotives and an unusual U-shaped hi line trestle on the right of the photo, 1920s. *Legacy of the Plains Museum Collection, Gering, Nebraska.*

The Union Pacific was a little late in arriving in the beet-growing areas of the North Platte Valley. Construction of the Union Pacific's North Platte Branch began at O'Fallons, Nebraska (16.5 miles west of North Platte), in 1907. The line reached Northport in 1909 and finally reached Gering in 1911. The line moved farther west to Haig, about seven miles northwest of Gering, in June 1913. An engine house was built there along with a wye to turn locomotives. The line continued on to the Nebraska-Wyoming state line in October of the same year. There was no farther western movement until May 1922, when a long forty-two mile extension brought the branch to Cottier, Wyoming. The line finally arrived at South Torrington in November 1925.

The Union Pacific and Great Western established beet dumps on the main line at different times. Dumps were located at places as far east as Keystone, In the region that is the subject of this book, there were dumps at Broadwater, Kelly, Towers, Northport, Mohler, South Bayard, McGrew, Melbeta, Gering, Haig, South Mitchell, Pelton, Balleyvue, South Morrill, Joyce and Lyman for the Great Western. Dumps in Wyoming on the main line to serve Holly at South Torrington included Canal, Stebbins, Huntley, Holly, Yoder, Veteran, Heldt, Cottier and Buffington.

The UP line running south from Yoder, Wyoming, was the first of the UP beet spurs being completed in September 1926. This 8.5-mile branch would not be a dead end for long, as it would be the beginning of the North Platte Cutoff that, proceeding south, would reconnect with the Union Pacific main line near Egbert, Wyoming. Beet dumps were located at Goodland, Shingie, Fonda and Creighton.

This spur/branch was vital to the establishment of the Holly factory at South Torrington. Without the dumps on the UP in the irrigated areas south of the North Platte River, the factory would probably have been built north of the river in or adjacent to the city of Torrington. The connection to South Torrington as well as the link between Creighton and Egbert are still very much in operation today, although most of the beet dumps are long gone.

Rumors of a spur south of Gering into the upper Gering Valley had circulated for several years. In an article in the fall of 1924, a story appeared under the heading "BUILD BEET SPUR TRACK NEXT YEAR....Nine miles proposed into the upper Gering Valley....No, it is not official, but it is a fact just the same. The Union Pacific will construct next spring the new railroad beet spur south and west from Gering into the upper valley, as has been discussed in these columns from time to time."[193]

It wasn't quite a fact yet, as it took another three years to finally happen in 1927. The Gering-Riford beet spur ran south from the wye (which is still there in 2020) east of the Gering factory on the main line south for about 3.5 miles to another wye, and the line split with a short stub east to the first dump at Mathers. The other leg goes due west for roughly another 3.5 miles with a dump at Moon about halfway.

The line then swung northwest for about two miles past a dump at Hilliker, then due west again to the end about another mile to the last dump on the spur at Riford. I have documentation that references another dump called "Roubadeau," which apparently was located between Moon and Hilliker at some time on this spur.

In Scott Bluff County along the UP spurs are facilities other than beet dumps. Based on old Union Pacific memos I acquired many years ago, there is confirmation that there was a stockyard with a double-deck loading chute at the Hilliker dump (confirmed in a UP memo dated June 4, 1957, confirming the retirement of the facility), which was probably used for loading sheep for the Swift packing plant in north-central Gering. Other facilities were located at Mathers, which was abandoned in late 1959, and Riford, according to a UP memo dated December 9, 1959. Additional details recently discovered confirm the past existence of double-deck livestock loading facilities at Janise, Mathers, Moon, Sears and Stegal, and a single-deck facility at Riford.

There was also at least one potato cellar and loading spot at Moon on the branch that was in operation in 1963 as per the lease dated January

Mathers beet dump south of Gering on the UP Gering beet spur. *Legacy of the Plains Museum Collection, Gering, Nebraska.*

Union Pacific work train on the Gering spur in the 1950s. (This is the only photo I have found of a train operating on one of the UP spurs in the valley.) *Virl "Red" Davis photo from the James L. Ehernberger Collection.*

15, 1964. This may have operated after the branch had been abandoned, as I have another document dated October 1, 1964, stating, "authority has been received for the retirement of the Gering Branch and the contract has been awarded to Western Builders of North Platte, Inc. for removal."[194]

Additional confirmation of some of this other activity was found in a magazine article in 2000 written by Arthur Stensvad, a UP fireman who operated on the branch for a while. "During 1963–64…we also made runs on the branch south out of Gering to Mathers, Moon, Roubadeau, Hilliker and Riford, a total of 9.8 miles. Business consisted of a couple of beet dumps, a couple of potato sheds and a sheep loading station at Riford."[195]

I have been unable to confirm the exact date this branch ceased operation, but based on the information from Art Stensvad's article, it appears to be about 1965.

The other UP beet spur ran south from Lyman and was built in two steps in consecutive years. The Lyman-to-Stegall branch runs south and then splits with the first leg built going east to Stegall. The junction is about 3.0 miles south of the wye, which is just east of the Lyman factory. It is located shortly after it passes the Sears dump 2.8 miles down the line. After the junction, the Hartman dump is about 1.5 miles farther east,

A wood trestle on the Lyman Sears section of the beet spur over Kiowa Creek. (This is the only remnant of the valley spurs that I can still find in 2019.) *Photo by the author.*

culminating at the Stegall dump about 6.4 miles from the start. This part of the spur was built in 1926.

The other branch of the spur proceeds directly south of the junction about 1.2 miles to the Bellinger dump and then on another 1.6 miles to the Janise dump. This branch of the spur was completed in 1927. This spur also had livestock loading facilities at both Hartman and Janise, as confirmed in the Stensved article. These two branches may have had traffic as late as March 1976, as they still show in an employee timetable issued that month. The Bellinger dump apparently had already been abandoned by then and the Lyman factory had long since been closed. The beets from the spur were brought to the Gering plant for processing in the years after that closure. One additional point of interest is that a wood trestle located on this branch crossing Kiowa Creek still stands in 2020 as one of the few reminders of the existence of any of these beet spurs.

8

THE BEET DUMPS

As mentioned earlier, beet dumps, both at the factories and even more so along the railroad main or spur lines, were critical to getting the crop to the processing plants. The earliest dumps were little more than literally dumping places for the beets on the ground, which were then painstakingly loaded by hand into waiting railcars of some type, as mentioned in an earlier chapter. This obviously was very inefficient and needed to be improved for both the speed of the loading and to minimize the loss of sugar content while the beets waited to be moved. This inefficiency led to the development of the first wood unloading trestles or hi lines.

The hi line trestles utilized a device called a Carroll Tilting Platform at the center of a long narrow wood trestle. The wagon or truck would be driven into position at the apex of the hi line next to the waiting railroad hopper cars, secured tightly in place on the platform, and then a winch would tilt the bed of the wagon or truck, dumping the beets to one side into a waiting railroad car.

This entire operation—taking the vehicle up the spindly hi line trestle, unloading the beets and then going down the other side of the trestle—was not for the faint-hearted, and from time to time things didn't go as planned and disaster would strike.

These wood unloading trestles were operated for a number of years. During the 1930s, they began to be fazed out and replaced with mechanical conveyers. The conveyers were called Hartburg piling machines. These

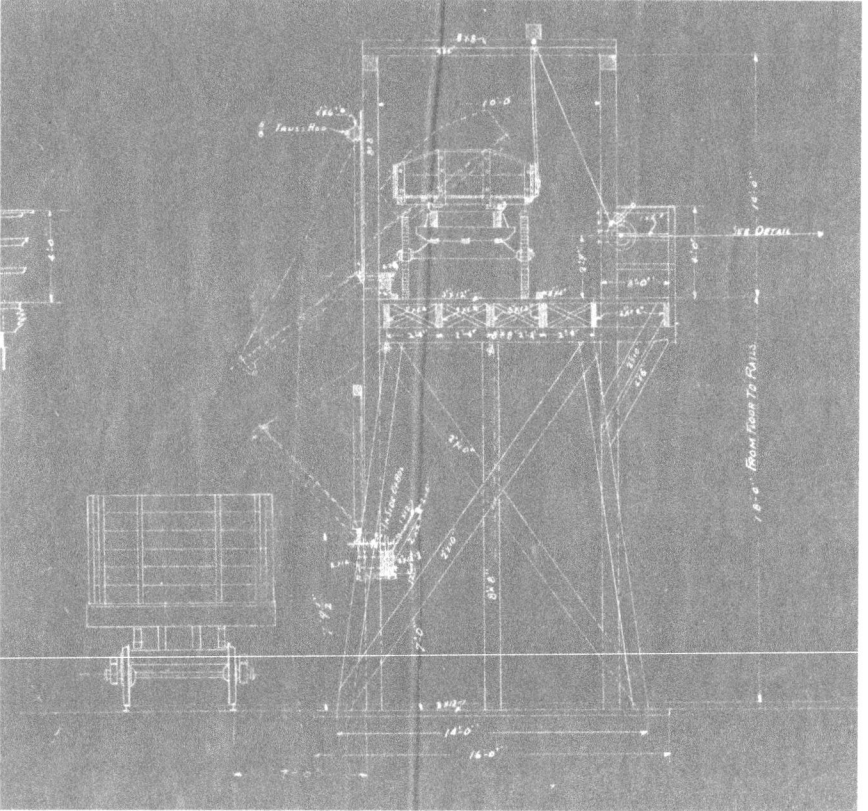

Top: A 1906 Great Western Sugar beet unloading hi line wood blueprint. *Western Sugar Co-op*.

Bottom: A 1906 Great Western Sugar beet unloading hi line wood trestle cross-section blueprint showing the Carroll tilting platform. *Western Sugar Co-op*.

conveyers still utilized small wood trestle-type platforms, but the beets were dumped into the conveyor loader in a fixed position.

This next change utilized a moveable conveyer, which would pile the beets on the ground if they were being delivered faster than there were railcars to load them into, and then they would be used to convey the beets up into the railcars from the ground.

Top: Haig beet dump wood hi line trestle in the 1920s. *Great Western Sugar Photo. Lucke family collection.*

Bottom: Haig beet dump wood hi line trestle in the 1920s showing the Carroll tilting platform in operation. *Great Western Sugar photo. Lucke family collection.*

This basic system is still used today at many of the remaining beet dumps, but now they are loaded into re-haul trucks and taken to the factory.

Although most of the rural rail beet dumps are long gone, several of the locations where they were established many years ago still are used today. This time they utilize the moveable conveyors to reload the beets from the

The wood hi line trestles always presented concern for the safety of those driving a wagon or truck to the top of the tilting platform. Sometimes, those fears were confirmed, as shown in this photo. *Legacy of the Plains Museum Collection, Gering, Nebraska.*

In more recent years (1965), some of the lower mechanical dumps were still in use, as seen at the Sears dump south of Lyman. *Photo courtesy of the Scotts Bluff County Assessor's Office.*

By the mid-1960s, some of the dumps were utilizing moveable loaders like these at Bayard. They have a scale platform for trucks to pull up on and dump, as shown on the left. *Henderson Collection at Legacy of the Plains Museum.*

Another type of loader at the Haig dump, 1930s. *Great Western Sugar photo. Lucke family collection.*

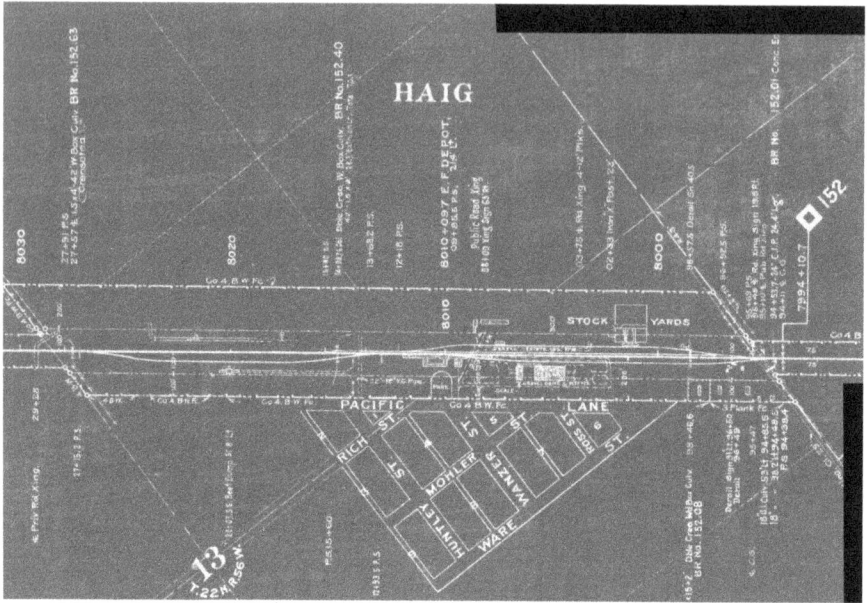

Haig dump map showing the beet dump in the center-left side of the railroad line, circa 1950. *Union Pacific line map. Author's collection.*

The "Towers" (Kemp) dump, two miles north of Northport on the CB&Q Alliance line, featured an earthen ramp to the unloading platform, mid-1960s. There, the beets were dumped and carried up on the conveyor and could be loaded into waiting trucks or moved farther up a second, smaller conveyor and loaded into railroad hopper cars. *Photograph by Kenneth R. Middleton.*

ground into large tractor trailer re-haul trucks. Several other dumps have been establised in the last few years at locations around the Wyo-Braska territory that better serve today's beet-producing areas in the valley and beyond. Much has changed over the years, but the basic proceedure of the beet dumps is still pretty much the same.

9

THE DINKIES

The small 0-4-0T (no lead wheels–four drive wheels–no trailing wheels tank type) saddle tank steam locomotives operated for many years in the North Platte Valley factories by Great Western Sugar were called "dinkies" because of their small size. (A saddle tank locomotive carried its water in a saddle-shaped tank that draped over the boiler of the locomotive, generally not in a separate trailing tender, as with most larger steam locomotives.) (As a side note, I have seen the term spelled two different ways: dinky or dinkey.) GW operated the first of these at Mitchell in 1924. It and the dinky for the Gering plant were the only two dinkies purchased new by Great Western. Both of these, and almost all of the others owned by GW, were manufactured by the Davenport Locomotive Works of Davenport, Iowa. Over the next fifty years or so, at least five different dinkies operated at the mill in Lyman, Mitchell, Scottsbluff, Gering and Bayard. I cannot find any record of one being used at the mill in Minatare, but that is still a possibility.

The first Davenport acquired by the sugar company was one of only two dinkies bought new by the GW. It went to Mitchell, Neb. plant in March, 1924, where it served until swapped with Scottsbluff around 1950. The other new model purchased by the Great Western went to Gering, Neb. in July 1939. The others were obtained second hand, mostly from construction companies and quarries in the Midwest.[196]

Why did these diminutive locomotives work so well for about a half century, and well beyond the retirements of most steam locomotives in the United States by nearly two decades? "After the beets come into the yard. The dinkies pull them—generally two hoppers at a time—through a 'Wet hopper' where hot water jets loosen the beets so that they fall out of the railroad cars and directly into the flume leading to the factory."[197]

What was so special about the dinkies performing this operation that newer diesel locomotives couldn't do? The wet hopper process sprayed heavy streams of water from above the hopper cars. A diesel locomotive generally would bring in air for its engine to operate from above. The steamy stream of water droplets from above would stall out most diesel locomotives, rendering them pretty useless for the operation. A not-so-minor secondary consideration is that the dinkies had long since been paid for and were therefore comparatively inexpensive for GW to operate as long as they did, provided they received appropriate regular maintenance. "The wet hopper system involves dumping beets directly from cars into hoppers under the tracks, from which the beets are flumed to the factory. The hoppers

The Gering dinky no. 2267 pulling two hopper cars through the wet hopper in the fall of 1966. *Virl "Red" Davis photo from the James L. Ehernberger Collection.*

This photo shows GW dinky no. 1988 at the then-closed Lyman factory in 1955. Of special note is the GW-built wood coal tender attached to the loco in the photo. *James L. Ehernberger photo.*

accommodate either 2 or 3 cars at a time. Small saddle-back locomotives are used for handling the cars."[198]

Let's look at their operations at each of the factories, starting at Lyman. The locomotive used here, no. 1988, was built in 1924 for the Costello Brothers in Knoxville, Tennessee, and was acquired by GW in February 1930. I assume it went directly to the recently completed Lyman factory and even operated there long after it had closed. It probably would have been used to sort cars coming in off of the Lyman beet spur for assembly into a train to be hauled to Gering. This operation apparently may have continued until 1963, when it was sent to Bayard. The accompanying photo shows it operating with a small GW-built wood coal tender, which would have allowed it to operate longer and at greater distances from the factory without the need of frequent coal reloading.

Next up, moving west to east with the GW valley mills, is the Mitchell dinky. The original Mitchell dinky, which was purchased new (no. 1990), operated at the Mitchell plant for a number of years but for some unknown reason was swapped with Scottsbluff at an undetermined date. Mitchell received engine no. 2003 (built in September 1924 for the Platte-Rogers Company in Pueblo, Colorado), which operated at that mill until retired about 1975. The engineer in the 1960 campaign photo is Eddie Whittington.

The Mitchell dinky no. 1990 on November 24, 1960, showing engineer Ed Whittington. *Photo courtesy of Darlene Robertson.*

This locomotive has apparently sported several different paint schemes over the years. In the 1965 photo, it is in basic black; in the 1973 photo, it is painted powder blue. In the current photo of the locomotive on display, it is in an attractive black with orange and gray trim. This dinky is preserved and on display at a park adjacent to the BNSF tracks on Main Street in Mitchell.

Next down the river east is the Scottsbluff factory. This factory has had at least two locomotives over the years in operation. Engine no. 2003, mentioned in the Mitchell paragraph, operated in Scottsbluff until swapped with Mitchell for engine no, 1990, which GW purchased new for the Mitchell mill in 1924. This locomotive was modified in Scottsbluff and was unique for GW in that "the Scottsbluff engine can roam around the vicinity of its beet dump hooked onto an 'Umbilical cord' which supplies it with natural gas. When its engineer needs to go beyond the length of the hose, the engine switches over to a propane tank."[199]

Most of the time, the small loco would be moving just a couple of cars around the factory or through the wet hopper or picking them up from the Burlington siding. This was not always the case, however.

Like the other dinkies in the valley, it operated until the mid-1970s. After retirement, it was sold for $3,000 to Ken Layher and moved to Wood River, Nebraska. He has restored it, and it was operable recently on his property.

The Mitchell dinky no. 1990 on October 1973, after the end of the campaign. *Photo by the author.*

The Mitchell dinky no. 1990 in static display at a park adjacent to the BNSF line on Main Street in Mitchell, July 2019. *Photo by the author.*

Top: Scottsbluff dinky no. 2003 moving a heavy load of four loaded beet hoppers past the limestone pile in the sugar factory yard, November 3, 1965. *Hol Wagner photo*.

Bottom: The Scottsbluff dinky no. 2003 moves loaded hopper cars through the wet hopper washer, October 1973. *Photo by the author*.

Based on personal observation, this is the only remaining valley dinky that can still operate today. The rest are on static display in various conditions.

Moving across the river south, we arrive at the Gering factory and its dinky. This locomotive, no. 2267, built new for Great Western in August 1938, was in operation at the Gering factory from July 1939 through about 1975.

A few years after ceasing operations, the Gering dinky was sold as well. It was moved by Ray Sample and was sold to a buyer in South Dakota.

The former Scottsbluff dinky no. 2003 as it appeared in 2019, in the possession of Ken Layher in Wood River, Nebraska. Of all the former GW dinkies from the valley, this is the only one that is still operable. *Photo courtesy of Ken Layher.*

The Gering dinky no. 2267 in operation on November 12, 1967. *Joe Hardy photo. Brian Garner collection.*

The Gering dinky no. 2267 in operation again, October 1973. *Photo by the author.*

When the Gering dinky no. 2267 was sold a few years later, it was loaded on a flatbed truck by Ray Sample. *Photo courtesy of Ray Sample.*

The Gering dinky no. 2267 is on static display at the 1880 Town in Midland, South Dakota. *Author's collection.*

It currently resides in Midland, South Dakota, in the 1880 Town. A poor attempt to backdate it to fit with the theme of the attraction includes the addition of a balloon stack. It, unfortunately, appears to be in poor condition.

As we move farther east to the next factory, we pass by Minatare. The only indication I have found about operation of a dinky there is in a picture of a dinky pulling hopper cars through a wet hopper. The picture, part of the Zemanek Collection at Legacy of the Plains Museum, identifies the location as Minatare, but I can find no information on the identification of which dinky it may have been. I have found no other information about dinky operations at that factory.

Moving on to the last mill in the valley, at Bayard, we find evidence of two dinkies. One of them, no. 1871, built in April 1921 for the Grand Rapids Gravel company in Michigan, was acquired by GW in February 1931. It operated at the mill in Wheatland, Wyoming, for a number of years until that mill closed. It was then sent to Bayard, where it may have operated for a time, but I cannot be certain. In the fall of 1973, I found it in back of the mill being cannibalized for parts.

The dinky that operated for many years in Bayard, no. 1988 came from the Lyman plant in 1963. Details on it are found above in the Lyman dinky

Unidentified dinky purportedly operating at the wet hopper at the Minatare sugar factory. *Zemanek Collection at Legacy of the Plains Museum Collection, Gering, Nebraska.*

Bayard dinky no. 1871 operated for a time at Wheatland, Wyoming. It was transferred to Bayard and may have operated there for a time. After that, it was placed on two stub rails in the back of the Bayard mill property, where it sat being cannibalized for parts for the other company locomotive. Shown in October 1973. *Photo by the author.*

information. Again, like the others, it was retired in the mid- to late 1970s. The Great Western donated this dinky to the city of Bayard, and in 1986, they raised about $800 to move it to Swimming Pool Park, where it resides to this day. It appears to be fairly well cared for but may be due for a new coat of paint soon.

Before we leave the details of the dinkies operated in the North Platte Valley by the Great Western Sugar Company, I notice one interesting fact in viewing the current photos of the dinkies in 2019, all of them except for the one beautifully restored and cared for by Ken Layher are missing their bells! I suspect someone decided that they would make great souvenirs after the dinkies were retired but before they were disposed of. The other possible explanation that I have heard is that the all-brass bells were removed and sold for scrap by unknown parties. Whatever the fate of the bells, this probably happened shortly after the dinkies' retirement. The photo of the Gering dinky being loaded onto a flatbed trailer shows that the bell was already missing.

Top, left: The Bayard dinky no. 1988 in operation, doing its job of pulling beet hopper cars through the wet hopper dump, October 1973. *Photo by the author.*

Top, right: A bell from one of the North Platte Valley GW dinkies donated by Darold Davidson Jr. *Photo by the author.*

Bottom: The Bayard dinky no. 1988 as it appears on static display in July 2019 in Swimming Pool Park on the north side of Bayard. *Photo by the author.*

As I was nearing the completion of this manuscript, I received an unexpected call from Darold Davidson Jr. of Scottsbluff. His father, Darold Davidson Sr., worked for Great Western from 1950 until 1986 as the district engineer. Word was out in the community that I was trying to track down a dinky bell to add to the collection at the Legacy of the Plains Museum in

Gering. Davidson's unexpected phone call shocked me when he said he had had one of the bells for over forty years from his dad and wanted to know if I was interested in picking it up for the museum. Needless to say, I picked it up in a few hours and presented it to the museum a short time later. I am not sure which valley dinky this one came from, but at least a little of the mystery of the disappearing bells has been solved.

10

THE SUGAR BEET INDUSTRY IN THE NORTH PLATTE VALLEY SINCE THE CONSTRUCTION PHASE

Much has transpired in the sugar beet industry in the valley and to the American sugar industry in general since the last factory in the valley was completed at Lyman in 1927. Years of boom and bust caused in part by government policies that manipulated the sugar import market and government production quotas, grower/processor disagreements, improvements in processing technology, improved crop transportation, the changing tastes of consumers and the usual good and bad crop years caused by the weather have taken their toll on beet processing in the North Platte Valley. Let's look closer at some of these as we summarize the story in this book.

The U.S. government has been involved with the domestic sugar industry almost since its infancy. During World War I, it encouraged expanded production to meet the demands of the world, especially war-torn Europe. After the war, with European production gradually resumed, production in the United States remained steady or even expanded as more factories were planned or built.

In spite of the recent slump in sugar prices the United States tariff commission believes that reasonable returns may be expected in the industry for a long time to come. The world is still about 2 million tons short of pre-war production because of the interruption caused by the war in central Europe. Before Germany, Austria-Hungary, Russia and France are able to return to their old scale of production the world's needs will have increased sufficiently to absorb all of the new acreage that can be put in in western Nebraska. The present satisfactory return to the sugar growers may be reduced in the not far distant future but not to such a point as to make the industry unprofitable. A dozen new factories may be erected in the western half of Nebraska in the next five years without endangering a dollar of the capital invested in them.[200]

This editorial ran shortly after construction had started on the Minatare mill, and just a few months before, the collapsing sugar market resulted in the suspension of construction of that factory. The dozen new factories never happened, although a few more were built, as we have learned in this book.

As the market struggled with the return of European production and increasing imports of cane sugar from Cuba, the Philippines and other places, things appeared to improve in the middle of the decade of the 1920s. Diseases such as beet curly top virus and insects became greater problems as acreage expanded at a rapid clip. Optimism for the industry's future was still prevalent.

Too well known to bear extended discussion are the benefits that follow the erection of a beet sugar factory, the development of a market for the new crops, the production of livestock by-product feeds, the increase in population, in revenues for governmental and school purposes, and the many other improvements which seem in a peculiar manner attached to such factory and railroad construction in the valley.[201]

One has only to look back to conditions in the valley before the advent of the sugar industry to appreciate the place it has made for itself in the communities.[202]

Disputes between growers and Great Western led to the intrigues in the mid-decade between Great Western and Holly in Wyo-Braska regarding who was in whose territory. The grower/processor disputes continued even until this day. With this situation in the background, the industry, as well as the world's economy, collapsed with the advent of the Great Depression in 1929. In an attempt to stabilize the markets for sugar, the government passed the Sugar Act of 1933. A processing tax on sugar as well as production quotas was set for the industry. These acreage quotas directly led to the short lifespans of the Minatare and Lyman factories, as the other factories absorbed the diminishing amount of sugar production acres. The government's

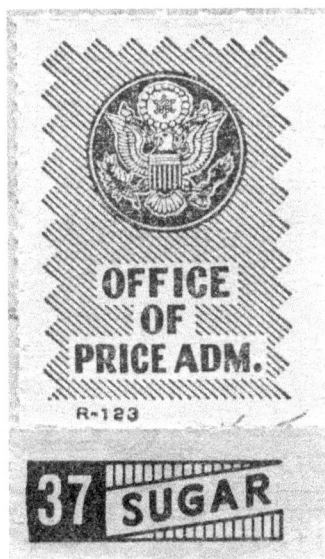

A seal for the Office of Price Administration and a sugar rationing stamp from World War II. *Author's collection.*

involvement in the sugar industry continued until about 1974, when the protection of the industry was allowed to expire.

When the Depression ended with the start of World War II, some decisions made by the government seem strange in retrospect. At a time when it would seem that market conditions similar to those during World War I would encourage all-out production to meet world demand, the restrictive quotas of the 1933 act continued, thus helping to create a sugar shortage and necessitating the rationing of sugar. "On January 24, 1942 OPA [the Office of Price Administration] was given the authority to ration sugar by the War Production board directive #1....Increased demand under wartime conditions plus decrease in world supply and transportation difficulties led to sugar rationing."[203]

To anyone who knows history, there was a great labor shortage during the war, as many able-bodied men had been drafted. This labor shortage was critical in agriculture, since so much of the production work was still labor-intensive. Even with this consideration, we must wonder why the restrictive quotas were maintained during the war when a less bureaucratic alternative might have been to maximize production, as had been done during World War I. This increased production and the corresponding increase in income would have greatly benefited sugar producers nationwide.

Conflicts between growers and food processors are as old as farmers selling crops for others to use beyond their own needs. The sugar beet industry was no different. Frequent conflicts occurred between what the growers thought their crop payment should be guaranteed and what the processor—the sugar company—was willing to offer. Many times, the disagreements led to threats of crop grower boycotts of sugar beet growing and thoughts of building grower-owned mills.

As the process of producing sugar from beets became more mechanized and faster, the need for so many sugar mills decreased. Bigger and more productive equipment eventually led to the situation we have in 2020 in the valley: only one factory still operating. For the 2020 crop, only the larger and much modernized Scottsbluff factory will operate. The mills at Lyman and Minatare are long gone. What remains of the mills at Gering, Mitchell, Bayard and now Torrington are utilized primarily for their bulk storage capacity. The goal of about a century ago, to have a mill operating in your valley town, has vanished as more can be processed with fewer facilities.

As roads improved in the valley, the need for many miles of beet spurs was reduced. Except for the comparatively few loads brought to the factory by growers, most all of the beets still go to rural dumps across the southern panhandle for transport to the factory in Scottsbluff by large tractor trailer re-haul trucks. The last of the spurs disappeared more than a quarter century ago and are only a part of the valley's history now.

One thing probably not foreseen in the 1920s was the increased use of artificial sweeteners and the invention of extracting sweeteners from corn. High-fructose corn sweeteners have replaced much of the use of sugar in soft drinks and many other food products. While recent medical studies seem to point to the corn sweeteners as a possible cause of greater obesity in the population, their lower cost has severely decreased the demand for beet (and cane) sugar.

Another factor affecting the beet sugar industry in the valley (and the rest of the domestic industry as well) is increased imports of low labor cost cane sugar from overseas. Without some protection to balance labor costs with these foreign competitors, the market for all domestic sugar, both beet and cane, is softened.

One final factor affecting both the valley sugar beet industry and all agriculture here is the unpredictability of the weather from one season to the next. Although most of the former sugar beet growing area is irrigated, timely spring rains before the water flows are still critical for those who still surface irrigate. Wide variations in spring and fall temperatures have a greater effect on the crop production for each season. This is one variable that no one in agricultural production of any kind can regulate. Despite all of our technology, agriculture is still very much at the mercy of the weather.

THE STATE OF THE INDUSTRY IN THE NORTH PLATTE VALLEY TODAY

The state of the sugar beet industry in the North Platte Valley in 2020 is one of change. After the closure of the final former processing plant in Torrington, the local growers are totally dependent on the recently modernized Scottsbluff mill. The other six mills in the valley are either gone completely or being used for sugar storage at most. This Scottsbluff mill, originally opened for the 1910 crop harvest, had a daily processing capacity of 1,200 tons per day at that time. By the 1930 crop year, the processing capacity of the seven mills in the valley was estimated to be approximately 11,300 tons per day. The current capacity of the Scottsbluff mill alone is 8,250 tons per day.

Although the processing is all in Scottsbluff now, production of the beets has expanded out from the valley over the years. A significant portion of the crop is now grown in the nearby counties of Kimball, Cheyenne, Box Butte, Sioux and Sheridan in Nebraska as well as in Platte and Laramie Counties in Wyoming. They are in addition to the original growers in Scotts Bluff, Morrill and Goshen Counties. Where it was once nearly impossible to grow beets in areas without surface irrigation, the preponderance of center pivot irrigation, which has exploded over the last forty years or so, has made it practical to produce beets in areas where only dry land crops could be grown in the past.

According to the U.S. Department of Agriculture, sugar made from sugar beets accounted for between 55 and 60 percent of all the sugar consumed in the United States in the early part of the twenty-first century. In 2004, Nebraska ranked sixth and Wyoming ranked seventh in sugar beet production among U.S. states. Combined, they produced 5.31 percent of U.S. production. (Ironically, Colorado, once the capital of sugar beet production in the High Plains, had fallen to eighth place, with only 1.95 percent of the total production at that time.)

The boom times of the early twentieth century for recruiting, building and operating a sugar factory in the valley is long past. The industry is no longer as dominant in the overall crop production picture of the area. It does, however, still represent a very significant cash crop for the farmers in the valley and the surrounding area. The sugar beet industry will likely remain an important part of the economy of the North Platte Valley for a long time to come.

The story I have attempted to tell in this book is one of a history of the sugar beets and community development in an area of about seventy-five miles east to west along the North Platte River. It is my hope that, by presenting this information in one place, it will be possible for future generations of researchers and residents to find answers to questions about the industry that pretty much built "The American Valley of the Nile"[204] in the first half of the twentieth century.

NOTES

Introduction

1. *Gering Courier*, editorial, November 1918.

Chapter 1

2. *Sugar Press*, April 1924, 8.
3. *Sugar Press*, 1922.

Chapter 2

4. *Sugar Press* (December 1925), 17.
5. Ibid., 17–18.

Chapter 3

6. *Norfolk News*, December 28, 1899, 9.
7. Ibid., October 7, 1904, 7.
8. *Omaha Bee*, editorial, December 12, 1904, 2.
9. *Norfolk News*, December 16, 1904, 1.

10. Ibid.

11. *Norfolk News*, January 27, 1905, 2.

12. *Omaha Bee*, February 2, 1899, 7.

13. Ibid., June 6, 1899, 1.

14. Ibid.

15. *Norfolk Weekly Journal*, May 14, 1909, 1.

16. Ibid., October 1, 1909, 8.

Chapter 4

17. Will M. Maupin, "The Beet Industry in Nebraska," *Sugar Press*.

Chapter 5

18. *Sugar Press*, May 1922.

19. Ibid.

20. N.C. Vandemoer, "Company Feeding at Scottsbluff," *Sugar Press*, January 1924, 11.

21. Ibid; Verne Huff, "Notes on Scottsbluff's Campaign."

22. *Sugar Press*, 1916.

23. *Gering Courier*, May 1, 1925.

24. Ibid.

25. Ibid., May 8, 1925.

26. Ibid., March 4, 1927.

27. Colorado & Southern Railroad, annual report, 1926.

28. *Gering Courier*, November 20, 1925.

29. Ibid., advertisement, February 24, 1928.

30. Ibid.

31. *Sugar Press*, Spring 1946, 6–7.

32. *Grand Old Days of Great Western*.

33. "What Are Beets Worth to a Community?," *Sugar Press*, June 1936.

34. *Sugar Press*, 1944.

35. Ibid.

36. *Gering Courier*, January 21, 1927.

37. Ibid.

38. "The Sugar Cities—Bayard," *Sugar Press*, May 1922, 35–36.

39. *Scottsbluff Star-Herald*, May 17, 1972.

40. *Bayard Transcript*, February 6, 1986.

41. *Mitchell Index*, November 20, 1919, 1.

42. Ibid.

43. Ibid.

44. Ibid.

45. Ibid

46. Ibid.

47. Ibid., December 18, 1919, 1.

48. Ibid.

49. Ibid., January 8, 1920, 1.

50. Ibid.

51. Ibid., February 26, 1920.

52. Ibid.

53. Ibid., March 11, 1920, front page.

54. Ibid., April 29, 1920, 1.

55. Ibid., May 6, 1920, 1.

56. Ibid.

57. Hamilton, *Footprints in the Sugar*, 510.

58. *Sugar Press* (April 1922): 2.

59. *Minatare Free Press*, January 16, 1920, front page.

60. Ibid.

61. Ibid., January 30, 1920, 1.

62. Ibid., May 28, 1920, 1.

63. Ibid., July 2, 1920, 1, quoting from an article by E.T. Westervelt in the *Scottsbluff Republican*.

64. Ibid.

65. Ibid.

66. Ibid., July 20, 1920, front page.

67. Ibid., December 16, 1920, front page.

68. *Minatare Free Press*, December 17, 1920, front page.

69. Ibid., December 24, 1920, front page.

70. Ibid., February 11, 1921, front page.

71. *Sugar Press*, October 1925, 12, statement of October 7, 1925, from J.D. Lippitt.

72. Ibid.

73. Ibid., October 8, 1925, 1.

74. Ibid.

75. Ibid., October 15, 1925, 1.

76. Ibid.

77. *Scottsbluff Star-Herald*, October 30, 1925, 1.

78. Ibid., October 31, 1925, 1.

79. *Minatare Free Press*, November 12, 1925, 1.

80. *Gering Courier*, quoting the *Denver Post*, November 11, 1925, 1.

81. *Scottsbluff Star-Herald*, November 29, 1925, 1.

82. *Minatare Free Press*, November 17, 1925, 1.

83. Ibid., November 17, 1925, 1.

84. *Gering Courier*, December 18, 1925, 1.

85. *Scottsbluff Star-Herald*, January 9, 1926, 1.

86. Ibid.

87. Ibid.

88. Ibid., January 17, 1926, 1.

89. Ibid.

90. Ibid., January 17, 1926, 6.

91. Ibid.

92. Ibid., January 20, 1926, 1.

93. Ibid.

94. Ibid.

95. Ibid., January 21, 1926, 1.

96. *Sugar Press*, November 1926, 17.

97. Ibid.

98. *Minatare Free Press*, May 8, 1941, 1.

99. Ibid.

100. *Scottsbluff Star-Herald*, May 9, 1941, 2.

101. *Minatare Free Press*, May 29, 1941, 1.

102. Inscription on the back of one of the photos from the Minatare Factory demolition set-Photographer unknown

103. *Scottsbluff Star-Herald*, August 27, 1920, 1.

104. *Gering Courier*, September 25, 1925, 1.

105. Ibid.

106. Ibid.

107. Ibid.

108. Ibid.

109. Ibid.

110. Ibid., September 25, 1925, 3.

111. Ibid., September 25, 1925, from the *Gering Midwest*.

112. Ibid., May 28, 1926

113. Ibid., August 20, 1926, 1.

114. *Sugar Press*, December 1926.

115. *Scottsbluff Star-Herald*, September 28, 1927, 3.
116. Ibid.
117. *Gering Courier*, October 7, 1927, 1.
118. Ibid.
119. *Scottsbluff Star-Herald*, June 18, 1949, 1.
120. Ibid.
121. *Goshen County Journal*, July 1, 1920, 1.
122. Ibid.
123. *Goshen County Journal*, July 8, 1920, 1.
124. Ibid., editorial, July 1, 1920, 2.
125. Ibid., August 26, 1920, 1.
126. Ibid., September 30, 1920, 1.
127. *Scottsbluff Star-Herald*, November 23, 1920, 6.
128. Ibid., from the *Lingle Review*, December 28, 1920, 1.
129. *Torrington Telegram*, from the *Denver Post*, January 18, 1923, 1.
130. Ibid., January 25, 1923, 1.
131. Ibid.
132. Ibid.
133. Ibid.
134. Ibid.
135. *Scottsbluff Star-Herald*, January 26, 1923, 1.
136. *Torrington Telegram*, February 15, 1923, 1.
137. Ibid.
138. Ibid., February 15, 1923, 1.
139. Ibid.
140. Ibid., March 10, 1923, 1.
141. Ibid., March 29, 1923, 1.
142. Ibid.
143. Ibid.
144. Ibid., April 12, 1923, 1.
145. Ibid., May 31, 1923, 1.
146. *Scottsbluff Star-Herald*, September 25, 1923, 7.
147. Ibid., February 29, 1924, 1, quoting from *Wheatland Times*.
148. Ibid.
149. *Goshen County Journal*, September 24, 1925, 1, from *Scottsbluff Star-Herald*.
150. *Torrington Telegram*, October 1, 1925, 1.
151. Ibid.
152. Ibid.
153. Ibid., October 8, 1925, 1.

154. Ibid.

155. Ibid., editorial, October 8, 1925, 4.

156. Ibid., October 15, 1925, 1.

157. *Goshen County Journal*, October 27, 1925, 1.

158. Ibid.

159. *Torrington Telegram*, December 3, 1925, 1.

160. Ibid., editorial, January 26, 1926, 6.

161. Ibid.

162. *Wind Pudding & Rabbit Tracks*.

163. Ibid.

164. Ibid.

165. *Torrington Telegram*, August 26, 1926, 1.

166. Ibid., October 14, 1926, 1.

167. *Gering Courier*, December 12, 1926, 1.

168. *Scottsbluff Star-Herald*, March 11, 2017. Article by Sandra Hansen Ag, editor, in the special "Pride" section.

Chapter 6

169. *Scottsbluff Star-Herald*, December 21, 1921, 4.

170. *Goshen County Journal*, October 27, 1925, 1, quoting from the *Scottsbluff Republican*.

171. Ibid.

172. *Scottsbluff Star-Herald*, August 3, 1927, 1.

173. *Bridgeport News-Blade*, August 4, 1927, 1.

174. Ibid., 2.

175. Ibid.

176. Ibid., August 11, 1927, 1.

177. *Scottsbluff Star-Herald*, October 12, 1927, 1.

178. Ibid.

179. *Bridgeport News-Blade*, October 6, 1927, 1.

180. Ibid.

181. Ibid., February 23, 1928, 1.

182. Ibid.

183. Ibid., April 5, 1928, 1.

Chapter 7

184. Wagner, "Beet Sugar Industry."
185. Kistler and Hardy, *Alliance and Everywhere West.*
186. Wagner, "Beet Sugar Industry."
187. Kistler and Hardy, *Alliance and Everywhere West.*
188. *Scottsbluff Star-Herald*, November 25, 1919, 1.
189. *Sugar Press,* July 1920, 34.
190. Ibid., August 1920, 33.
191. Ibid., September 1920, 29.
192. Ibid., November 1920, 44.
193. *Gering Courier*, October 17, 1924, 1.
194. R.W. Holland, Union Pacific memo, Omaha, October 1, 1964.
195. Stensvad, "Working the Sugar Beet Tramps."

Chapter 9

196. Morgan, *Sugar Tramp.*
197. Ibid.
198. *Sugar Press,* August 1930, 24.
199. Morgan, *Sugar Tramp.*

Chapter 10

200. *Scottsbluff Star-Herald*, editorial, September 16, 1920, from the *Nebraska State Journal.*
201. *Gering Courier*, September 25, 1925, 3.
202. Ibid.
203. Society of Ration Token Collectors, "United States Rationing in World War II," 25.
204. *Scottsbluff Star-Herald*, editorial, October 5, 1923, 5.

BIBLIOGRAPHY

Books and Magazines

Annual Report of the Colorado & Southern Railroad. 1926.

Ehernberger, James L. "The North Platte Branch and Cut-Off Operations." *Streamliner Magazine* 23, no. 2 (Spring 2009).

Grand Old Days of Great Western. Longmont, CO: Great Western Sugar Company, 1959.

Hamilton, Candy. *Footprints in the Sugar.* Ontario, OR: Hamilton-Bates Publishers, 2009.

Kistler, Richard, and Joseph Hardy. *Alliance and Everywhere West.* David City, NE: South Platte Press, 1990.

Morgan, Gary. *Sugar Tramp: Colorado's Great Western Railway.* Centennial, CO: Centennial Publications, 1975.

Society of Ration Token Collectors. *United States Rationing in World War II.* Gettysburg, PA: Society of Ration Token Collectors, 1999.

Stensvad, Arthur E. "Working the Sugar Beet Tramps." *Streamliner Magazine* 14, no. (Spring 2000).

Sugar Press. Great Western Sugar Company. Various issues.

Through the Leaves. Great Western Sugar Company. Various issues.

Wagner, Hol. "The Beet Sugar Industry and the Burlington." *Burlington Bulletin* 32 (July 1996).

Wind Pudding & Rabbit Tracks. Goshen County History Book Committee. Homesteaders Museum, Torrington, Wyoming.

Newspapers

Bayard (NE) Transcript
Bridgeport (NE) News-Blade
Gering Courier (Scottsbluff, NE)
Goshen County (WY) Journal
Minatare (NE) Free Press
Mitchell (NE) Index
Norfolk (NE) News
Norfolk (NE) Weekly Journal
Omaha Bee
Scottsbluff (NE) Star-Herald
Torrington (WY) Telegram

ABOUT THE AUTHOR

The author was born in Brooklyn, New York, in 1948. He grew up on Long Island, graduating from East Rockaway High School in 1966. He enlisted in the United States Marine Corps a few weeks later and achieved the rank of lance corporal in his two years' enlistment. Thirteen months of his active duty was spent with the First Marine Air Wing at Da Nang and Chu Lai in Vietnam. After his active duty was honorably completed, he moved to Scottsbluff, Nebraska, to attend Hiram Scott College. He received a bachelor of arts degree in political science with a history minor in August 1971. He later received a second BA degree in business administration from Chadron State College in 1978. He met his wife, Nita, shortly after arriving in western Nebraska. They have been married for over fifty years and have one son, Lawrence Matthew, an Emmy Award–winning director at KUSA Channel 9 in Denver, Colorado.

After graduation, he worked in an antipoverty program for several years. He worked for House of Hose, a hydraulic hose and coupling manufacturer, for a few years in the old Great Western Sugar Company office in Lyman, Nebraska, as operations manager. In 1981, he took the plunge and opened a retail hobby shop, Oregon Trail Hobbies, in Gering, achieving one of his lifelong dreams. He successfully operated the shop for nearly twenty-five years.

He ran for city council in Gering in the late 1970s, was elected and served a total of thirty-four years on that body after being reelected numerous times. While on the council, he served on many boards, including two years as president of Twin Cities Development and four years as president of Panhandle Resource Conservation and Development Board. He is a past member of the Gering Planning Commission and the board of adjustment.

In other activities, he has served as a 4H county fair judge in agricultural engineering for over twenty years in about half a dozen counties. He was also president of the Nebraska Numismatic Association in 1979–80. He is a member of the First Marine Air Wing Association Vietnam Service, the Veterans of Foreign Wars, the American Legion and the Vietnam Veterans of America. He currently serves on the board of directors of the Legacy of the Plains Museum near Scottsbluff National Monument and is currently the chairperson of the Gering LB840 economic development committee